THE CREDIT DISPUTE LETTER BIBLE

John D. Harris

ISBN:1530481309
ISBN-13:9781530481309

Content

Credit Repair is very specialized in many situations. If you need personal guidance on a specific issue you can call me. My phone number and information is on **PAGE 156.**

My Experience: Finance Degree, 6 years loans officer at a national bank, 4 1/2 years credit bureau manager for one of the big three credit bureau's   John D. Harris

LET'S GET STARTED

Ok, Let's start at the beginning. Recently you have probably found out your credit is not the greatest. It might not be your fault or it might be.

Your looking around the internet trying to get someone to repair your credit or perhaps you are smart and want to do it yourself.

I first started working in the credit business many years ago. My first job was working as a loans officer for a national bank. My job was to get financing for people with very shaky credit.

Much of my pay was commission based. This really drove me to help people get the loans they needed. The only way to do this was to rapidly increase their credit score.

At first this seemed impossible but after a chance encounter with a man named Tom Bradley things started to change.

Tom worked at a national credit bureau and we met at a business convention about mortgages.

Tom showed me many techniques on (TM)Rapid Rescoring and Quick Credit Repair Techniques.

Well because of my success at funding these hard to get loans I was given a promotion to loans manager.

Me and Tom stayed in touch and a few years before he retired he got me a job at his credit bureau. When I first got there I was very surprised at how high up in the company he was. He took me under his wing and that's when school got kicked into high gear.

We worked 9 hour days and every second Saturday. Talk about a lesson on the credit industry. He showed me things that would be the difference between someone losing their house or not. It was very powerful stuff.

I could go on and on here about my experience working as a credit bureau manager or how I was a loans officer for 6 years but I won't bore you with all the details.

This really is not about me anyways. It's about you and your credit. You can choose to believe me or not..

Credit Repair is very specialized in many situations. If you need personal guidance on a specific issue you can call me. My phone number and information is on **PAGE 156.**
 My Experience: Finance Degree, 6 years loans officer at a national bank, 4 1/2 years credit bureau manager for one of the big three credit bureau's   John D. Harris

Those credit bureau's destroy people's lives. They track everything about everyone and they don't let people know how they are calculating scores. It's so stupid. They sell your information to everyone willing to pay. They tell everyone they can't change their scores.

They tell you to just forget about that house or car or better job. Or they make you pay crazy interest rates.

I got so sick and tired of seeing these stupid scores ruining people's lives. Don't get me wrong the bureau I was working for paid me a lot of money.

After a while though I couldn't live with myself, it became harder and harder to get a good night's sleep.

Well it's your lucky day. You are about to get the insider information to boost your fico score through the roof.

Good credit is essential in America today, and there is a network of credit reporting agencies that keep track of your current credit rating and check your credit worthiness every time you apply for a loan, credit card or any other type of credit.

If you feel overwhelmed and confused by your credit situation, this proven credit repair system will amaze you. You will learn exactly what credit dispute letters to use and why.

it's tough to know who to believe. There are so many people making ridiculous claims, it's insane. It's like day after day, you get hit with hype pitch after hype pitch.

In a moment, I'll tell you specifically what I can do for you. But first, here is why you should believe me to begin with:

Here are 4 good reasons to believe what I say:

One: I've been in this business for a very long time. My kind of experience is very rarely matched. Many bankers and even credit bureau professionals do not know many of these techniques.

Two: I am not asking you for some large investment that is going to make me rich and you poor.

Three: I hate the credit bureaus. They track our every move, they should be illegal. Working for one I learned all their little secrets.

Four: How many of these people selling these books have been on the inside. My guess is none after reading the garbage in most of these books.

I'll show you the steps for removing negative items from your credit report using the secrets, tips, and techniques that credit repair companies use to repair credit.

Due to your lack of credit knowledge, they can charge hundreds of dollars for something that you can, and should, do yourself for a few bucks, sometimes even free.

Bad credit is big business and companies reap millions of dollars every year from people's lack of knowledge about their credit and FICO score! How?... With extremely high interest rates, huge down payments, fees, late charges, and penalties.

Credit Repair is very specialized in many situations. If you need personal guidance on a specific issue you can call me. My phone number and information is on **PAGE 156.**

My Experience: Finance Degree, 6 years loans officer at a national bank, 4 1/2 years credit bureau manager for one of the big three credit bureau's   John D. Harris

The Fact Is: You don't need a lawyer to eliminate your debts!

In Fact: You don't need a credit counselor to fix your credit for you!

In Fact: You don't need any kind of so-called professional to help you at all!

Never be denied or rejected because of credit problems again.

Get the mortgage or car loan you want with a low rate and low payments – Credit won't be an issue.

Get the best loans only made available to the "elite" with an excellent credit rating.

Get qualified for business loans in a snap.

Clear up all your bad credit troubles FOREVER.

This is the step–by-step, easy to follow system attorneys and credit repair specialists use to remove negative items from your credit report – PERMANENTLY!

You will have secrets you need to know in order to raise your credit scores by up to 200 points

You will learn small changes you can make right now to take your credit from good to EXCELLENT

Discover the real secret behind getting negative items removed from your credit without committing fraud. Use the Credit Dispute Letters the Pro's Use.

The First Question I get from everyone wanting to repair their credit is:

Should I use a law firm to Send Dispute Letters and Repair my Credit?

My Answer is always Absolutely NO. Here's why.

These so called law firms don't care about your credit at all.

You pay them monthly.

Do they really want your credit to get better. Then they lose the monthly income.

This would not make any financial sense at all. They want to delay any credit repair as long as possible.

They will try and string you along by getting an inquire or two removed. The average customer will stay paying the monthly fee for 6 months.

They are dispute mills that don't work

You do all the work and they send out some generic credit dispute letter

The credit bureaus know these companies and get thousands of letters from them.

Credit Repair is very specialized in many situations. If you need personal guidance on a specific issue you can call me. My phone number and information is on **PAGE 156.**
My Experience: Finance Degree, 6 years loans officer at a national bank, 4 1/2 years credit bureau manager for one of the big three credit bureau's   John D. Harris

They file them under frivolous challenges.(or like we used to say under "G' for garbage lol) I know I used to do it.

If you got thousands of form letters from a company every day wouldn't you send them back a form letter.

We at the bureau knew the law firms just wanted the longest delay possible. Why? So they can make the most money of course.

It is sort of like one hand washes the other. Unfortunate but absolutely true!

If you use one of these so called law firms you will see little if any response from the credit reporting agencies. In a few months you will have realized you have wasted your time and money.

Did You Know That:

•   There are 3 National Credit bureau's

•   They do not share information.   Credit bureaus are businesses. It is not in their best interest to share information with competitors (other bureau's). This is one big advantage to you.

•   Credit bureau's all compile their own score for you. This is commonly called your FICO score.

- FICO stands for Fair Isaac Company. This company developed the software that the 3 main bureau's use to calculate your credit score.

- When you purchase a big item such as a car or house the financial institute will pull your credit from all 3 bureau's and take your middle score as your FICO score.

Most banks and large financial institutes report late payments etc with all 3 bureau's. Most smaller companies only report to one. This is due to cost restrictions. Most smaller companies are under a contract with a particular bureau. For example if you don't pay a phone bill it will most likely only show up on one bureau's report.

- Your FICO score is a formula that can be manipulated to your advantage if you know how the formula is calculated.

Credit Repair is very specialized in many situations. If you need personal guidance on a specific issue you can call me. My phone number and information is on **PAGE 156.**
 My Experience: Finance Degree, 6 years loans officer at a national bank, 4 1/2 years credit bureau manager for one of the big three credit bureau's   John D. Harris

WHAT IS CREDIT

Credit is borrowed money that you can use to purchase goods and services when you need them. You get credit from a credit grantor, whom you agree to pay back the amount you spent, plus applicable finance charges, at an agreed-upon time.

There are four types of credit:

1.   Revolving credit. With revolving credit, you are given a maximum credit limit, and you can make charges up to that limit. Each month, you carry a balance (or revolve the debt) and make a payment. Most credit cards are a form of revolving credit.

2.   Charge cards. While they often look like revolving credit cards and are used in the same way, charge accounts differ in that you must pay the total balance every month.

1.   **Service credit.** Your agreements with service providers are all credit arrangements. You receive electricity, cellular phone service, gym membership, etc., with the agreement that you will pay for them each month. Not all service accounts are reported in your credit history.

2.   **Installment credit.** With installment credit, a creditor loans you a specific amount of money, and you agree to repay the money and interest in regular installments of a fixed amount over a set period of time. Car loans and mortgages are two examples of installment credit.

History of Credit

The idea of exchanging goods or services in return for a promise of future payment developed only after centuries of trade: money and credit were unknown in the earliest stages of human history. Nevertheless, as early as 1300 B.C., loans were made among the Babylonians and Assyrians on the security of mortgages and advance deposits. By 1000 B.C., the Babylonians had already devised a crude form of the bill of exchange, so a creditor merchant could direct the debtor merchant in a distant place to pay a third party to whom the first merchant was indebted. Installment sales of real estate were being made by the Egyptians in the time of the Pharaohs.

Traders in the Mediterranean area, including Phoenicia, Greece, Rome and Carthage, also used credit. The vast boundaries of the Roman Empire, at the beginning of the Christian era, encouraged widespread trading and a broader use of credit. In the disorganized period that marked the decline and fall of the Roman Empire, credit bills of exchange or promissory notes were widely used to reduce the dangers and difficulties of transferring money through unorganized trading areas.

During the Middle Ages, a period which spanned 1000 years from about 500 to 1500 A.D., credit bills were essential to the trading activities of the prosperous Italian city-states. Lending and borrowing, as well as buying and selling on credit, became widespread practices; the debtor-creditor relationship was found in all classes of society from peasants to nobles, even including the Pope and other high dignitaries of the Church. A common form of investment and credit, especially in Italy, was the "sea loan" whereby the capitalist advanced money to the merchant and thus shared the risk. If the voyage was a success, the creditor got the investment back plus a substantial bonus of 20 to 30 percent; if the ship was lost, the creditor could lose the entire sum.

Another form of credit was the "fair letter" which was developed at the fairs held regularly in the centers of trading areas during the Middle Ages. The fair letter amounted to a promissory note to be paid before the end of the fair or at the time of the next fair. It enabled a merchant, who was short of cash, to secure goods on credit. This gave the merchant time either to sell the goods brought to the fair or to take home and sell the goods that had been purchased on credit.

Credit in Early America

The discovery of the New World provided new opportunities for the growth of capitalism and the expansion of credit. The first recorded use of open credit in early America took place with the establishment of the first permanent colony in New England. In September 1620, the Mayflower set sail from England for Virginia. Because of bad weather and navigational errors, the Pilgrims ended up off the coast of Cape Cod and eventually established the village of Plymouth in Massachusetts. While the journey itself was a tremendous achievement, so was its financing.

The Pilgrims had spent three years of arduous negotiations in England attempting to raise the funds necessary for the trip. A wealthy London merchant financed the trip and provided for "all credit advanced and to be advanced." In return, the Pilgrims contracted to work for a period of seven years. At the end of that period, payment would be made to the creditors based on the size of the individual investment.

The original credit of £1,800 could not be paid at the end of seven years, so an alternative arrangement was agreed upon: £200 to be paid annually for a term of nine years. This arrangement had to be renegotiated and finally, after 25 years, the last payment was made. This was the first example of credit in early America.

To finance the American Revolution, the Second Continental Congress made efforts to finance the Army of the United Colonies. The Congress had only three alternatives: borrow the money from sympathetic countries abroad which was an impossible task since the Colonist's credit in the world stood at zero; impose taxes which was unpopular and the very cause that had brought about the American Revolution; or issue bills of credit.

In June of 1775, the Continental Congress authorized the printing of $2,000,000 in various denominations ranging from one dollar to eight dollars. Trouble for the Continental currency began almost at once; each note had to be hand signed which was not a simple task considering 49,000 of them had to be signed. Counterfeiting of the currency was rampant. The principle behind the Continental currency was, in essence, a promise to pay the final bearer, at some point in the future, the face value in Spanish coins, the coins in widest circulation at this time.

In 1783, the Treaty of Paris was signed bringing an official end to the war and official recognition of the United States by England. Trading resumed and American importers and wholesalers extended generous terms to their customers. Generally, sales were made on terms of 12 months but even where six- or nine-month terms where offered, it was not uncommon for an account to remain unpaid for a much longer period, up to 24 months or more.

With the restoration of pre-Revolutionary trade customs and habits, credit references assumed importance, although in most instances, proper information was still lacking. Some prospective purchasers took the precaution of using the names of prominent people

Credit Repair is very specialized in many situations. If you need personal guidance on a specific issue you can call me. My phone number and information is on **PAGE 156.**
My Experience: Finance Degree, 6 years loans officer at a national bank, 4 1/2 years credit bureau manager for one of the big three credit bureau's   John D. Harris

they knew when placing orders on credit. Credit references accompanied orders, however in most cases, merchants took their chances.

Terms of sale, as they developed during the 1800s, reflected the changes in the rapidly expanding economy. The 12-month period, which had prevailed, showed a tendency to become shorter. By the 1830s, the average term of sale was about six months.

Hard financial times hit the country in the mid 1830's. The population was rapidly growing and business was expanding. The sale of land on credit went virtually unchecked. The banking system was not centralized. By the summer of 1837, bank after bank closed its doors and thousands of businesses went into bankruptcy. The financial panic of 1837 saw the beginnings of the Mercantile Agency, established in 1841 by Lewis Tappan. It was this credit information agency which eventually became Dun & Bradstreet and helped transform credit, and with it, the course of American commerce.

The story of American credit, as we now know it, was not solely influenced by Dun & Bradstreet. Another organization important for credit managers worldwide was formed in 1896 in Toledo, Ohio. A group of credit executives, representing a hundred or so of their colleagues, organized themselves into a national association for credit managers, the National Association of Credit Men. Their exchange of credit information was initially conducted on a local and regional level. The association expanded into the National Association of Credit Management (NACM), which today with its network of Affiliated Associations, represents approximately 30,000 credit executives worldwide.

HISTORY OF CREDIT CARDS

As far back as the late 1800s, consumers and merchants exchanged goods through the concept of credit, using credit coins and charge plates as currency. It wasn't until about half a century ago that plastic payments as we know them today became a way of life.

Early beginnings

In the early 1900s, oil companies and department stories issued their own proprietary cards, according to Stan Sienkiewicz, in a paper for the Philadelphia Federal Reserve entitled "Credit Cards and Payment Efficiency." Such cards were accepted only at the business that issued the card and in limited locations. While modern credit cards are mainly used for convenience, these predecessor cards were developed as a means of creating customer loyalty and improving customer service.

The first bank card, named "Charge-It," was introduced in 1946 by John Biggins, a banker in Brooklyn, according to MasterCard. When a customer used it for a purchase, the bill was forwarded to Biggins' bank. The bank reimbursed the merchant and obtained payment from the customer.

The catches: Purchases could only be made locally, and Charge-It cardholders had to have an account at Biggins' bank.

In 1951, the first bank credit card appeared in New York's Franklin National Bank for loan customers. It also could be used only by the bank's account holders.

The Diners Club Card was the next step in credit cards, the story began in 1949 when a man named Frank McNamara had a business dinner in New York's Major's Cabin Grill.

When the bill arrived, Frank realized he'd forgotten his wallet. He managed to find his way out of the pickle, but he decided there should be an alternative to cash. McNamara and his partner, Ralph Schneider, returned to Major's Cabin Grill in February of 1950 and paid the bill with a small, cardboard card. Coined the Diners Club Card and used mainly for travel and entertainment purposes, it claims the title of the first credit card in widespread use.

Plastic debuts

By 1951, there were 20,000 Diners Club cardholders. A decade later, the card was replaced with plastic. Diners Club Card purchases were made on credit, but it was technically a charge card, meaning the bill had to be paid in full at the end of each month.

According to its archivist, American Express formed in 1850. It specialized in deliveries as a competitor to the U.S. Postal Service, money orders (1882) and traveler's checks, which the company invented in 1891. The company discussed creating a travel charge card as early as 1946, but it was the launch of the rival Diners Club card that put things in motion.

In 1958 the company emerged into the credit card industry with its own product, a purple charge card for travel and entertainment expenses.

In 1959, American Express introduced the first card made of plastic (previous cards were made of cardboard or celluloid).
American Express soon introduced local currency credit cards in other countries. About 1 million cards were being used at about 85,000 establishments within the first five years, both in and out of the U.S. In the 1990s, the company expanded into an all-purpose

card. American Express, or Amex as it often is called, is about to celebrate its 50th credit card anniversary.

Closed-loop System

The Diners Club and American Express cards "functioned in what is known as a 'closed-loop' system, made up of the consumer, the merchant and the issuer of the card," Sienkiewicz writes. "In this structure, the issuer both authorizes and handles all aspects of the transaction and settles directly with both the consumer and the merchant."

In 1959, the option of maintaining a revolving balance was introduced, according to MasterCard. This meant cardholders no longer had to pay off their full bills at the end of each cycle. While this carried the risk of accumulating finance charges, it gave customers greater flexibility in managing their money.

Bank Card Associations

"The general-purpose credit card was born in 1966, when the Bank of America established the BankAmerica Service Corporation that franchised the BankAmericard brand (later to be known as Visa) to banks nationwide.

In 1966, a national credit card system was formed when a group of credit-issuing banks joined together and created the InterBank Card Association.

The ICA is now known as MasterCard Worldwide, though it was temporarily known as MasterCharge. This organization competes directly with a similar Visa program.

The new bank card associations were different from their predecessors in that an 'open-loop' system was now created, requiring interbank cooperation and funds transfers.

Visa and MasterCard's organizations both issue credit cards through member banks and set and maintain the rules for processing. They are both run by board members who are mostly high-level executives from their member banking organizations.

As the bank card industry grew, banks interested in issuing cards became members of either the Visa association or MasterCard association. Their members shared card program costs, making the bank card program available to even small financial institutions. Later, changes to the association bylaws allowed banks to belong to both associations and issue both types of cards to their customers.

Credit Card Processing Evolves

As credit card processing became more complicated, outside service companies began to sell processing services to Visa and MasterCard association members. This reduced the cost of programs for banks to issue cards, pay merchants and settle accounts with cardholders, thus allowing greater expansion of the payments industry.

Visa and MasterCard developed rules and standardized procedures for handling the bank card paper flow in order to reduce fraud and misuse of cards. The two associations also created international processing systems to handle the exchange of money and information and established an arbitration procedure to settle disputes between members.

Other Issuers Join the Party

Although American Express was among the first companies to issue a charge card, it wasn't until 1987 that it issued a credit card allowing customers to pay overtime rather than at the end of every month. Its original business model focused on the travel and entertainment charges made by business people, which involved significant revenue from merchants and annual membership fees from customers. While these products are still in its tool chest, the company has developed numerous no-annual fee credit cards offering low introductory rates and reward programs, similar to as traditional bank cards.

Another relatively recent entry into the card business is Discover Card, originally part of the Sears Corporation. According to Discover, its first card was unveiled at the 1986 Super Bowl. Discover Card Services sought to create a new brand with its own merchant network, and the company has been successful at developing merchant acceptance.

A 2004 antitrust court ruling against Visa and MasterCard -- initiated by the U.S. government and the Department of Justice -- changed the exclusive relationship that Visa and MasterCard enjoyed with banks. It allows banks and other card issuers to provide customers with American Express or Discover cards, in addition to a Visa or MasterCard.

The future

While the plastic card has been the standard for a half century, recent developments show alternative forms of payment rising to prominence, from online services such as PayPal to chips that can be implanted into cell phones or other devices.

Credit Repair is very specialized in many situations. If you need personal guidance on a specific issue you can call me. My phone number and information is on **PAGE 156.**
My Experience: Finance Degree, 6 years loans officer at a national bank, 4 1/2 years credit bureau manager for one of the big three credit bureau's   John D. Harris

The Main Axis Players

Yes they are the axis and you should treat them like they are the enemy.

There are 4 players on the axis side

Experian

Experian is a global information services group with operations in 40 countries, with corporate headquarters in Dublin, Republic of Ireland and operational headquarters in Nottingham, United Kingdom; Costa Mesa, California, United States; São Paulo, Brazil; and Heredia, Costa Rica.

The company now employs 17,000 people. It is listed on the London Stock Exchange and is a constituent of the FTSE 100 Index. Experian is a partner in the UK government's Verify ID system.

In the UK during the 1970s, GUS plc, a retail conglomerate with millions of customers paying for goods on credit, employed John Peace, a computer programmer at the time, to combine the mail order data from various GUS businesses and create a central database to which was later added electoral roll data as well as county court judgements. GUS's database was commercialized in 1980 under the name Commercial Credit Nottingham (CCN). In 1996 GUS plc acquired the US credit reporting business Experian, formerly known as TRW Information Services, from Bain Capital and the Thomas H. Lee Partners[4] and merged it into CCN.

During the next ten years, Experian broadened its product range to new industry sectors, beyond financial services, and entered new markets such as Latin America, Asia Pacific and Eastern Europe. The business expanded through both organic development and acquisitions. In October 2006 Experian was demerged from the British company GUS plc and listed on the London Stock Exchange.

In August 2005, Experian accepted a settlement with the Federal Trade Commission (FTC) over charges that Experian had violated a previous settlement with the FTC. The FTC's allegations concerned customers who signed up for the "free credit report" at Experian's Consumerinfo.com site. The FTC alleged that ads for the "free credit report" did not adequately disclose that Experian would automatically enroll customers in Experian's $79.95 credit-monitoring program.

In January 2008, Experian announced that it would cut more than 200 jobs at its Nottingham office as it moved development work to India to reduce costs.

Experian shut down its Canadian operations on 14 April 2009.

Experian's principal lines of business are credit services, marketing services, decision analytics and consumer services. The company collects information on people, businesses, motor vehicles and insurance. It also collects 'lifestyle' data from on- and off-line surveys.

Experian provides services in North America, Latin America, UK and Ireland, Europe, Middle East and Africa and Asia Pacific and reports its financial performance across those regions. Activities in these regions are grouped into four principal activities: credit services, decision analytics, marketing services and consumer services.

Like the other major credit reporting bureaus, Experian is chiefly regulated in the United States by the Fair Credit Reporting Act (FCRA). The Fair and Accurate Credit Transactions Act of 2003, signed into law in 2003, amended the FCRA to require the credit reporting companies to provide consumers with one free copy of their credit report per 12-month period. Like its main competitors, TransUnion and Equifax, Experian markets credit reports directly to consumers. Experian heavily markets its for-profit credit reporting service, FreeCreditReport.com, and all three agencies have been criticized and even sued for selling credit reports that can be obtained at no cost.

Experian refuses to follow California law with respect to disputes and relies only on the Fair Credit Reporting Act.

The company's largest operation is Experian North America, a consumer credit reporting agency that is considered one of the three largest American credit agencies along with Equifax and TransUnion.

Credit Repair is very specialized in many situations. If you need personal guidance on a specific issue you can call me. My phone number and information is on **PAGE 156.**

My Experience: Finance Degree, 6 years loans officer at a national bank, 4 1/2 years credit bureau manager for one of the big three credit bureau's   John D. Harris

Equifax

Equifax Inc. is a consumer credit reporting agency in the United States, considered one of the three largest American credit agencies along with Experian and TransUnion. Founded in 1899, Equifax is the oldest of the three agencies and gathers and maintains information on over 400 million credit holders worldwide.

Based in Atlanta, Georgia, Equifax is a global service provider with US $2.3 billion in annual revenue and 7,000+ employees in 14 countries. Equifax is listed on the NYSE.

Equifax was founded in Atlanta, GA, as Retail Credit Company in 1899. The company grew quickly and by 1920 had offices throughout the US and Canada. By the 1960s, Retail Credit Company was one of the nation's largest credit bureaus, holding files on millions of American and Canadian citizens.

Even though they still did credit reporting the majority of their business was making reports to insurance companies when people applied for new insurance policies including life, auto, fire and medical insurance. All of the major insurance companies used RCC to get information on health, habits, morals, use of vehicles and finances.

They also investigated insurance claims and made employment reports when people were seeking new jobs. Most of the credit work was then being done by a subsidiary, Retailers Commercial Agency.

Retail Credit Company's extensive information holdings, and its willingness to sell them to anyone, attracted criticism of the company in the 1960s and 1970s. These included that it collected "...facts, statistics, inaccuracies and rumors... about virtually every phase of a person's life; his marital troubles, jobs, school history, childhood, sex life, and political activities." The company was also alleged to reward its employees for collecting negative information on consumers.

As a result, when the company moved to computerize its records, which would lead to much wider availability of the personal information it held, the US Congress held hearings in 1970.

These led to the enactment of the Fair Credit Reporting Act in the same year which gave consumers rights regarding information stored about them in corporate databanks. It is alleged that the hearings prompted the Retail Credit Company to change its name to Equifax in 1975 to improve its image.

The company later expanded into commercial credit reports on companies in the US, Canada and the UK, where it came into competition with companies such as Dun & Bradstreet and Experian. The insurance reporting was phased out. The company also had a division selling specialist credit information to the insurance industry but spun off this service, including the Comprehensive Loss Underwriting Exchange (CLUE) database as ChoicePoint in 1997. The company formerly offered digital certification services, which it sold to GeoTrust in September 2001.

In the same year, Equifax spun off its payment services division, forming the publicly listed company Certegy, which subsequently acquired Fidelity National Information Services in 2006. Certegy effectively became a subsidiary of Fidelity National Financial as a result of this reverse acquisition merger.

For most of its existence, Equifax has operated primarily in the business-to-business sector, selling consumer credit and insurance reports and related analytics to businesses in a range of industries. Business customers include retailers, insurance firms, healthcare providers, utilities, government agencies, as well as banks, credit unions, personal and specialty finance companies and other financial institutions.

Equifax sells businesses credit reports, analytics, demographic data, and software. Credit reports provide detailed information on the personal credit and payment history of individuals, indicating how they have honored financial obligations such as paying bills or repaying a loan. Credit grantors use this information to decide what sort of products or services to offer their customers, and on what terms.

Equifax also provides commercial credit reports, similar to Dun & Bradstreet, containing financial and non-financial data on businesses of all sizes. Equifax collects and provides data through the NCTUE, an exchange of non-credit data including consumer payment history on telco and utility accounts.

From 1999, Equifax began offering services to the credit consumer sector in addition, such as credit fraud and identity theft prevention products. Equifax, and other credit monitoring agencies are required by law to provide US residents with one free credit file disclosure every 12 months; the Annualcreditreport.com website incorporates data from US Equifax credit records.

Credit Repair is very specialized in many situations. If you need personal guidance on a specific issue you can call me. My phone number and information is on **PAGE 156.**

My Experience: Finance Degree, 6 years loans officer at a national bank, 4 1/2 years credit bureau manager for one of the big three credit bureau's   John D. Harris

TransUnion

TransUnion is an American company that provides credit information and information management services to approximately 45,000 businesses and approximately 500 million consumers worldwide in 33 countries. It is also the third-largest credit bureau in the United States.

Like major competitors Equifax and Experian, TransUnion markets credit reports directly to consumers. The company is based in Chicago, Illinois, and its revenue in 2014 was US$1.3 billion.

TransUnion was originally formed in 1968 as a holding company for the railroad leasing organization, Union Tank Car Company. The following year, it acquired the Credit Bureau of Cook County, which possessed and maintained 3.6 million card files. In 1981, a Chicago-based holding company The Marmon Group acquired TransUnion for approximately $688 million.

Almost thirty years later, in 2010, Goldman Sachs Capital Partners and Advent International acquired it from Madison Dearborn Partners In 2014, TransUnion acquired Hank Asher's data company TLO. On June 25, 2015, TransUnion became a publicly traded company for the first time, trading under the symbol TRU.

TransUnion has evolved its business over the years to offer products and services for both businesses and consumers. For businesses, TransUnion has evolved its traditional credit score offering to include trended data that helps predict consumer repayment and debt behavior. This product, referred to as CreditVision, launched in Oct. 2013.

Its SmartMove™ service facilitates credit and background checks for consumers who may be serving in a landlord capacity.

In September 2013, the company acquired eScan Data Systems of Austin to provide post-service eligibility determination support to hospitals and healthcare systems. The technology was integrated into TransUnion's ClearIQ platform that tracks patients demographic and insurance related information to support benefit verification.

In November 2013, TransUnion merged with TLO LLC, a company that leverages data in support of its investigative and risk management tools. Its TLOxp technology aggregates data sets and using a proprietary algorithm to uncover relationships between data that were not possible before.

As part of its fraud protection products, it also offers business a tool called DecisionEdge that aggregates the data needed to prevent fraud through a system that customizes the information needed to finalize a transaction.

For consumers, TransUnion offers credit monitoring and identity theft protection tools. The company's app offers a function called CreditLock that allows an individual to unlock and lock their credit to help protect against fraudulent activity.

In 2003, Judy Thomas of Klamath Falls, Oregon, was awarded $5.3 million in a successful lawsuit against TransUnion. The award was made on the grounds that it took her six years to get TransUnion to remove incorrect information in her credit report.

In 2006, after spending two years trying to correct erroneous credit information that resulted from being a victim of identity theft, a fraud victim named Sloan filed suit against all three of the USA's largest credit agencies. TransUnion and Experian settled out of court for an undisclosed amount. In Sloan v. Equifax, a jury awarded Sloan $351,000. She wrote letters. She called them. They saw the problem. They just didn't fix it.

TransUnion has also been criticized for concealing charges. Many users complained of not being aware of a $17.95/month charge for holding a TransUnion account.

In March 2015, following a settlement with the New York Attorney General, TransUnion, along with other credit reporting companies, Experian and Equifax, agreed to help consumers with errors and red flags on credit reports. Under the new settlement, credit-reporting firms are required to use trained employees to respond when a consumer flags a mistake on their file.

These employees are responsible for communicating with the lender and resolving the dispute.

Credit Repair is very specialized in many situations. If you need personal guidance on a specific issue you can call me. My phone number and information is on **PAGE 156.**

My Experience: Finance Degree, 6 years loans officer at a national bank, 4 1/2 years credit bureau manager for one of the big three credit bureau's   John D. Harris

Fico

FICO (NYSE: FICO) is a software company based in San Jose, California and founded by Bill Fair and Earl Isaac in 1956. Its FICO score, a measure of consumer credit risk, has become a fixture of consumer lending in the United States.

In 2013, lenders purchased more than 10 billion FICO scores and about 30 million American consumers accessed their scores themselves.

FICO was founded in 1956 as Fair, Isaac and Company by engineer William Fair and mathematician Earl Isaac. The two had met while working at the Stanford Research Institute in Menlo Park, California. Selling its first credit scoring system two years after the company's creation, FICO pitched its system to fifty American lenders.

FICO went public in 1986 and is traded on the New York Stock Exchange. The company debuted its first general-purpose FICO score in 1989. Scores are based on credit reports and range from 300 to 850. Lenders use the scores to gauge a potential borrower's creditworthiness.

Fannie Mae and Freddie Mac first began using FICO scores to help determine which American consumers qualified for mortgages bought and sold by the companies in 1995.

FICO is headquartered in San Jose, California and has additional US locations in Roseville, Minnesota; San Diego; San Rafael, California; Fairfax, Virginia; New York City and Austin, Texas.

The company has international office locations in Australia, Brazil, Canada, China, Germany, India, Italy, Japan, Korea, Lithuania, Malaysia, the Philippines, Russia, Singapore, South Africa, Spain, Taiwan, Thailand, Turkey and the United Kingdom.

Thing to know

1) There are 3 different credit bureaus. TransUnion, Equifax and Experian.

2) All of these companies have different reports on you. This is because they don't share information on you with each other. They are competitors with each other. Each wants their own information, it's how they make money.

3) These CRA's (credit reporting agencies **are not affiliated with the government**. They are private companies.

4) They make money by selling your information to businesses who want to see if

you are credit worthy. Think of it like you own a furniture shop. You want to make more sales and extend credit. You don't know the customers personally. You are willing to pay $5 to find out if this customer pays other merchants back.

5) They use FICO to determine a score for each person. They pay FICO (Fair Isaac and Company) for their mathematical formula.

Where do the Credit Reporting Agencies Get there information

In the U.S., consumer reporting agencies collect and aggregate personal information, financial data, and alternative data on individuals from a variety of sources called data furnishers with which the reporting agencies have a relationship.

Data furnishers are typically creditors, lenders, utilities, debt collection agencies (credit bureaus) and the courts (i.e. public records) that a consumer has had a relationship or experience with. Data furnishers report their payment experience with the consumer to the credit reporting agencies.

The data provided by the furnishers as well as collected by the bureaus are then aggregated into the consumer reporting agency's data repository or files. The resulting information is made available on request to customers of the consumer reporting agencies' for the purposes of credit risk assessment, credit scoring or for other purposes such as employment consideration or leasing an apartment.

Given the large number of consumer borrowers, these credit scores tend to be mechanistic. To simplify the analytical process for their customers, the different consumer reporting agencies can apply a mathematical algorithm to provide a score the customer can use to more rapidly assess the likelihood that an individual will repay a particular debt given the frequency that other individuals in similar situations have defaulted.

Credit Repair is very specialized in many situations. If you need personal guidance on a specific issue you can call me. My phone number and information is on **PAGE 156.**

My Experience: Finance Degree, 6 years loans officer at a national bank, 4 1/2 years credit bureau manager for one of the big three credit bureau's   John D. Harris

What's on Your Credit Report

Although each credit reporting agency formats and reports this information differently, all credit reports contain basically the same categories of information.

Your social security number, date of birth and employment information are used to identify you. These factors are not used in credit scoring. Updates to this information come from information you supply to lenders.

Identifying Information.
Your name, address, Social Security number, date of birth and employment information are used to identify you. These factors are not used in credit scoring. Updates to this information come from information you supply to lenders.

Trade Lines.
These are your credit accounts. Lenders report on each account you have established with them. They report the type of account (bankcard, auto loan, mortgage, etc), the date you opened the account, your credit limit or loan amount, the account balance and your payment history.

Credit Inquiries.
When you apply for a loan, you authorize your lender to ask for a copy of your credit report. This is how inquiries appear on your credit report. The inquiries section contains a list of everyone who accessed your credit report within the last two years.

The report you see lists both "voluntary" inquiries, spurred by your own requests for credit, and "involuntary" inquires, such as when lenders order your report so as to make you a pre-approved credit offer in the mail.

Public Record and Collections.
Credit reporting agencies also collect public record information from state and county courts, and information on overdue debt from collection agencies. Public record information includes bankruptcies, foreclosures, suits, wage attachments, liens and judgments.

Prepaid Debit Cards, Checking Accounts, and Traditional Debit Cards

None of these aforementioned items appear on your credit reports. Debit cards and checking accounts are really the same thing, as a debit card is like a plastic version of a paper check.

And, a prepaid debit card is really not much more than a reloadable gift card with fees.

None of the three items are a true extension of credit, as you're only able to spend money that is already either: A) loaded on the card, or B) deposited in an account with a bank or credit union.

There is considerable confusion over the prepaid debit card and credit reporting issue because some of the companies and individuals who are paid to endorse these cards suggest they will help your credit reports and scores, which isn't at all true.

In fact, the credit bureaus now have language in their reporting standards guide that addresses the issue of prepaid debit cards and credit reporting.

It reads, "Do not report prepaid credit cards/gift cards because the consumer has no credit obligation."

There is, however, one scenario when your checking account could bleed into your credit report: If you have overdraft protection in the form of an unused installment loan that loan can be reported to the credit bureaus.

I personally have one of these on my credit reports and have had it for many years.

Evidence That You Are Now Married

When you get married nobody in the credit industry knows about it.

The credit reporting agencies don't know about it, your credit scores don't know about it, and lenders don't know about it.

There is nothing on a credit report that appears or changes just because you've gotten married.

Now, if you choose to apply jointly with your new spouse or you otherwise co-mingle your existing debt obligations and liabilities, then eventually your credit reports will look similar to your spouse's credit reports because the data will be so similar.

Want some great advice?

Maintain credit independence even after you're married.

There's no reason to co-mingle your debts and there's no reason to jointly apply for credit, except in the instance where you'll need two incomes to qualify for a loan.

Wealth Metrics

There's nothing on a credit reports that indicates your salary, your net worth, your debt-

to-income ratio, or the amount of money in your wallet, 401K, IRA, SEP, Money Market, brokerage account, or any other savings account.

There is no way to presume someone's income by looking at his or her credit reports.

This shouldn't be a surprise because credit reports are supposed to tell a story about your creditworthiness, not your income.

Income and other wealth metrics are measurements of capacity, or your ability to pay a bill. Credit reports and credit scores are supposed to tell a story about whether or you'll choose to pay your bills.

Public Utilities and Medical Bills
While there are exceptions to this rule most of the time your public utilities and medical bills do not appear on your credit reports month after month like a credit card or auto loan obligation.

If you do see a public utilities or medical bills on a credit report, they are likely there because they've gone into default and are being "worked" by a collection agency.

When a utility or medical bill goes into default, the service provider will normally outsource the collection of that bill to a debt collector.

And, debt collectors commonly report liabilities to the credit reporting agencies.

How is your Credit Score (FICO) calculated

The credit score, commonly referred to as a FICO score, is a proprietary tool created by the Fair Isaac Corporation. This is not the only way to get a credit score, but the FICO score is the measure that is most commonly used by lenders to determine the risk involved in a particular loan.

Due to the proprietary nature of the FICO score, the Fair Isaac company does not reveal the exact formula it uses to compute this number. However, what is known is that the calculation is broken into five major categories with varying levels of importance. These categories, with weight in brackets, are payment history (35%), amount owed (30%), length of credit history (15%), new credit (10%) and type of credit used (10%).

All of these categories are taken into account in your overall score - no one area or incident determines your score.

The payment history category reviews how well you have met your prior obligations on various account types.

It also looks for previous problems in your payment history such as bankruptcy, collections and delinquency. It takes into consideration the size of these problems, the time it took to resolve them, and how long it has been since the problems appeared. The more problems you have in your credit history, the weaker your credit score will be.

The next largest component is the amount that you currently owe to lenders. While this category focuses on your current amount of debt, it also looks at the number of different accounts and the specific types of accounts that you hold. This area is focused on your present financial situation, and a large amount of debt from many sources will have an adverse effect on your score.

The other categories (length of credit history, new credit and type of credit used) are fairly straightforward.

The longer you have a good credit history, the better. Common sense dictates that someone who has never been late with payment over twenty years is a much safer bet than someone who has been on time for two.

Also, people who apply for credit a lot probably already have financial pressures causing them to do so, so each time you apply for credit, your score gets dinged a little. And finally, a person with only one credit card is less risky than a person with 10, so the more types of credit accounts you have, the lower your score will be.

It is important to understand that your credit score only looks at the information contained on your credit report and does not reflect additional information that your lender may consider in its appraisal. For example, your credit report does not include such things as current income and length of employment.

Credit Repair is very specialized in many situations. If you need personal guidance on a specific issue you can call me. My phone number and information is on **PAGE 156.**
My Experience: Finance Degree, 6 years loans officer at a national bank, 4 1/2 years credit bureau manager for one of the big three credit bureau's   John D. Harris

Category	Description	Weight[5]
Payment history	how timely and consistent your payments are	40%
Depth of credit	length of credit history and types of credit previously received	21%
Utilization	debt-to-credit ratios and how much credit is available	20%
Balances	what your total debt is, most likely; delinquent debt is counted more harshly than current debt	11%
Recent credit	how recent and many new hard inquiries and new accounts there are	5%
Available credit	how much credit can be accessed, for example, could you spend $50,000 of credit tonight or within the next week	3%

Credit Score Ranges

There are several types of FICO credit score: classic or generic, bankcard, personal finance, mortgage, installment loan, auto loan, and NextGen score.

The generic or classic FICO score is between 300 and 850, and 37% of people had between 750 and 850 in 2013. According to FICO, the median classic FICO score in 2006 was 723, and 711 in 2011. The U.S. median classic FICO score 8 was 713 in 2014.
The FICO bankcard score and FICO auto score are between 250 and 900. The FICO mortgage score is between 300 and 850. Higher scores indicate lower credit risk.

Each individual actually has more than 49 credit scores for the FICO scoring model because each of three national credit bureaus, Equifax, Experian and TransUnion, has its own database.

Data about an individual consumer can vary from bureau to bureau. FICO scores have different names at each of the different credit reporting agencies: Equifax (BEACON), TransUnion (FICO Risk Score, Classic) and Experian (Experian/FICO Risk Model). There are four active generations of FICO scores:

1998 (FICO 98), 2004 (FICO 04), 2008 (FICO 8), and 2015 (FICO 9 Consumers can buy their classic FICO Score 8 for Equifax, TransUnion, and Experian from the FICO website (myFICO), and they will get some free FICO scores in that moment (FICO Mortgage Score 2 (2004), FICO Auto Score 8, FICO Auto Score 2 (2004), FICO Bankcard Score 8, and FICO Bankcard 2 (2004). Consumers also can buy their classic FICO score for Equifax (version of 2004; named Score Power) in the website of this credit bureau, and their classic FICO Score 8 for Experian on its website.

NextGen Risk Score

The NextGen Score is a scoring model designed by the FICO company for assessing consumer credit risk. This score was introduced in 2001, and in 2003 the second generation of NextGen was released. In 2004, FICO research showed a 4.4% increase in the number of accounts above cutoff while simultaneously showing a decrease in the number of bad, charge-off and Bankrupt accounts when compared to FICO traditional. FICO NextGen score is between 150 and 950.

Each of the major credit agencies markets this score generated with their data differently:

Experian: FICO Advanced Risk Score
Equifax: Pinnacle
TransUnion: FICO Risk Score NextGen (formerly Precision)

Prior to the introduction of NextGen, their FICO scores were marketed under different names:

Experian: FICO Risk Model
Equifax: BEACON
TransUnion: FICO Risk Score, Classic (formerly EMPIRICA)

Credit Repair is very specialized in many situations. If you need personal guidance on a specific issue you can call me. My phone number and information is on **PAGE 156.**

My Experience: Finance Degree, 6 years loans officer at a national bank, 4 1/2 years credit bureau manager for one of the big three credit bureau's   John D. Harris

VantageScore

VantageScore is the name of a credit rating product that was created by the three major credit bureaus (Equifax, Experian, and TransUnion). The product was unveiled by the three bureaus on 14 March 2006. The VantageScore is an attempt to compete with the FICO score produced by FICO.

VantageScore vs FICO

VantageScore and FICO score are different credit scores. FICO and the credit bureaus have allowed the public to know some information about the credit score categories and the corresponding calculation weights. FICO allows consumers get their generic or classic FICO score for Experian, TransUnion, and Equifax from myFICO website.

Consumers can get their VantageScores from free credit report websites for a fee, and TransUnion and Experian offer their VantageScore to consumers through their websites. All three agencies use the same formula to calculate the VantageScore; however, there are still discrepancies between the resulting scores if run for each of the credit reports.

This is due to different data the three agencies have on the credit reports. FICO, the original creator of the FICO Score, was not involved with the creation of VantageScore's new formula.

The three agencies have advertised the VantageScore as something that will help banks and lenders further drill down into the "subprime" categories. Subprime lenders are banks or other lenders dedicated to borrowers with less than perfect credit or harder to substantiate credit

The old VantageScore goes from 501 to 990, as reported by TransUnion:

A: 900–990
B: 800–899
C: 700–799
D: 600–699
F: 501–599

The VantageScore 3.0, the newest version, is between 300-850 from 2013.

While the exact details of how the score is calculated are unknown, VantageScore has released the categories and proportions used.

What contributes to a positive score in each category, and to what degree particular data affect the score, is unknown.

The score is meant to indicate the likelihood that a customer will pay the loan back on time and in a consistent manner; values which show behavior contrary to these are more likely to worsen the score, and vice versa.

Other Credit Scores

The non-FICO scores are called FAKO scores by some consumers. Experian has a credit score for educational use only (Plus Score) between 330 and 830, and Experian Scorex PLUS score is between 300 and 900. Equifax has the Equifax Credit Score between 280 and 850.

Some lenders use an Application Score between 100 and 990, and Credit Optics Score by ID Analytics Inc. between 1 and 999.

TransUnion's TransRisk New Account Score in the website Credit Karma is between 300 and 850, and Experian National Equivalency Score in Credit Sesame and Credit.com ranges from 360 to 840.

Several websites (TransUnion, Equifax, Credit Karma, Credit Sesame etc.) offer different credit scores to consumers but are not used by lenders. Innovis, ChexSystems and PRBC are other companies that produce credit scores used by some lenders.

Credit Repair is very specialized in many situations. If you need personal guidance on a specific issue you can call me. My phone number and information is on **PAGE 156.**
My Experience: Finance Degree, 6 years loans officer at a national bank, 4 1/2 years credit bureau manager for one of the big three credit bureau's   John D. Harris

YOUR ALLIES

What is the "Fair Credit Reporting Act"

The Fair Credit Reporting Act, 15 U.S.C. § 1681 ("FCRA") is U.S. Federal Government legislation enacted to promote the accuracy, fairness, and privacy of consumer information contained in the files of consumer reporting agencies.

It was intended to protect consumers from the willful and/or negligent inclusion of inaccurate information in their credit reports. To that end, the FCRA regulates the collection, dissemination, and use of consumer information, including consumer credit information.

Together with the Fair Debt Collection Practices Act ("FDCPA"), the FCRA forms the foundation of consumer rights law in the United States.

It was originally passed in 1970, and is enforced by the US Federal Trade Commission, the Consumer Financial Protection Bureau and private litigants.

The Fair Credit Reporting Act, as originally enacted, was title VI of Pub.L. 91–508, 84 Stat. 1114, enacted October 26, 1970, entitled An Act to amend the Federal Deposit Insurance Act to require insured banks to maintain certain records, to require that certain transactions in United States currency be reported to the Department of the Treasury, and for other purposes.

It was written as an amendment to add a title VI to the Consumer Credit Protection Act, Pub.L. 90–321, 82 Stat. 146, enacted June 29, 1968.

Consumer Reports

Commonly referred to as credit reports, a consumer report "contains information about your credit - and some bill repayment history - and the status of your credit accounts.

This information includes how often you make your payments on time, how much credit you have, how much credit you have available, how much credit you are using, and whether a debt or bill collector is collecting on money you owe. Credit reports also can contain rental repayment information if you are a property renter.

It also can contain public records such as liens, judgments, and bankruptcies that provide insight into your financial status and obligations.

The FCRA Regulates

The FCRA regulates:

Consumer reporting agencies;
Users of consumer reports; and,
Furnishers of consumer information.
If a consumer's rights under the FCRA are violated, they can recover:

Actual or statutory damages;
Attorney's fees;
Court costs; and,
Punitive damages if the violation was willful. "The threat of punitive damages under 1681n of the FCRA is the primary factor deterring erroneous reporting by the reporting industry."

The statute of limitations requires consumers to file suit prior to the earlier of: two years after the violation is discovered; or, five years after the violation occurred.

Consumer attorneys often take these cases on a contingency fee basis because the statute allows a consumer to recover attorney's fees from the offending party.

Users of Consumer Reports

Users of the information for credit, insurance, or employment purposes (including background checks) have the following responsibilities under the FCRA:

Users can only obtain consumer reports for permissible purposes under the FCRA;

Users must notify the consumer when an adverse action is taken on the basis of such reports; and,
Users must identify the company that provided the report, so that the accuracy and completeness of the report may be verified or contested by the consumer.

Employment Background checks

Employers using consumer reports to screen job applicants or employees must follow specific procedures, including:

Get your written permission;
Tell you how they want to use your credit report;
Not misuse your information;
Give you a copy of your credit report if the employer decides not to hire or fires you; and,
Give you an opportunity to dispute the information contained within your credit report before making a final adverse decision.

Credit Repair is very specialized in many situations. If you need personal guidance on a specific issue you can call me. My phone number and information is on **PAGE 156.**
My Experience: Finance Degree, 6 years loans officer at a national bank, 4 1/2 years credit bureau manager for one of the big three credit bureau's   John D. Harris

Furnishers of Information

A creditor, as defined by the FCRA, is a company that furnishes information to consumer reporting agencies. Typically, these are creditors, with which a consumer has some sort of credit agreement (such as credit card companies, auto finance companies and mortgage banking institutions).

Other examples of information furnishers are collection agencies (third-party collectors), state or municipal courts reporting a judgment of some kind, past and present employers and bonders. Lenders have an important role to play in ensuring credit reports are accurate. Under the FCRA, creditors who furnish information about consumers to consumer reporting agencies must:

Provide complete and accurate information to the credit reporting agencies;
Investigate consumer disputes received from credit reporting agencies;
Correct, delete, or verify information within 30 days of receipt of a dispute; and,
Inform consumers about negative information which is in the process of or has already been placed on a consumer's credit report within one month.
(This notice doesn't have to be sent as a separate notice, but may be placed on a consumer's monthly statement. If sent as part as the monthly statement, it needs to be conspicuous, but need not be in bold type. Required wording (developed by the US Federal Treasury Department):

Notice before negative information is reported: We may report information about your account to credit bureaus. Late payments, missed payments, or other defaults on your account may be reflected in your credit report.

Notice after negative information is reported: We have told a credit bureau about a late payment, missed payment or other default on your account. This information may be reflected in your credit report.

Consumer Reporting Agencies

Consumer reporting agencies (CRAs) are entities that collect and disseminate information about consumers to be used for credit evaluation and certain other purposes, including employment. Credit bureaus, a type of consumer reporting agency, hold a consumer's credit report in their databases. CRAs have a number of responsibilities under FCRA, including the following:

CRAs must maintain reasonable procedures to ensure the maximum possible accuracy of the information contained within a consumer's report;

Provide a consumer with information about him or her in the agency's files and take steps to verify the accuracy of information disputed by a consumer;

If negative information is removed as a result of a consumer's dispute, it may not be reinserted without notifying the consumer in writing within five days; and,

Remove negative information seven years after the date of first delinquency (except for bankruptcies (10 years) and tax liens (seven years from the time they are paid).

The three big CRAs—Experian, TransUnion, and Equifax—do not interact with information furnishers directly as a result of consumer disputes. They use a system called **E-Oscar.**
In some areas of the country, however, there are other credit bureaus.

Nationwide Specialty Consumer Reporting Agencies

In addition to the three big CRAs, the FCRA also classifies dozens of other information technology companies as "nationwide specialty consumer reporting agencies" that produce individual consumer reports used to make credit determinations. Under Section 603 of the Fair Credit Reporting Act, the term "nationwide specialty consumer reporting agency" means a consumer reporting agency that compiles and maintains files on consumers on a nationwide basis relating to:

Medical records or payments;
Residential or tenant history;
Check writing history;
Criminal background; and,
Other public record information.

Because these nationwide specialty consumer reporting agencies sell consumer credit report files, they are required to provide annual disclosures of their report files to any consumer who requests disclosure. A partial list of companies classified as nationwide specialty consumer reporting agencies under FCRA includes: Telecheck, ChoicePoint, Acxiom, Integrated Screening Partners, Innovis, the Insurance Services Office, Tenant Data Services, LexisNexis, Retail Equation, Central Credit, Teletrack, the MIB Group, United Health Group (Ingenix Division), and Milliman.

Although the major CRAs Experian, Equifax, and TransUnion are required by law to provide a central source website for consumers to request their reports, the nationwide specialty consumer reporting agencies are not required to provide a centralized online source for disclosure. The FCRA Section 612 merely requires nationwide specialty consumer reporting agencies to establish a streamlined process for consumers to request consumer reports, which shall include, at a minimum, the establishment by each such agency of a toll-free telephone number for such consumer disclosure requests.

Credit Repair is very specialized in many situations. If you need personal guidance on a specific issue you can call me. My phone number and information is on **PAGE 156.**
My Experience: Finance Degree, 6 years loans officer at a national bank, 4 1/2 years credit bureau manager for one of the big three credit bureau's   John D. Harris

What the CRA's Should Do

This is what Credit Bureaus should do when they receive a Dispute Letter.

An employee at the Credit Bureau receives the dispute and personally reviews it. During this review they gather information and documents in regards to the disputed account by contacting the original creditor or collection agency (Data Furnisher).

The Credit Bureau Employee then reviews copies of original documents like the Credit Application, Billing Statements, Billing and Payment Statements or notes in the account looking for any errors in reporting. If anything is in question they will request proof from the "Data Furnisher."

Once a full investigation has been completed, the Credit Bureau Employee will then update the consumer's account according to the results of the investigation.

This is great and Santa will bring your presents this year. This never happens.

Here's What Really Happens With Disputes

Credit bureaus use "Optical Character Recognition" or OCR which is part of their e-OSCAR system. This technology allows them to scan the consumer's letters and convert them into plain text that can be stored into a database. This way, they can deal with the over 20,000 dispute letters that they receive each day.

Your Credit Has Been Outsourced

Thanks to this technology and overseas outsourcing, credit bureaus have reduced that cost of each dispute from around $4.50 down to around 90 cents.

When the letter is received by the Credit Reporting Agency (Credit Bureau) it's electronically scanned with "Optical Character Recognition" and Matched against a DATABASE or "Boiler Plate" of Dispute Letters commonly used by Credit Repair Companies or found in cheap software programs and Credit Repair Books. If the algorithms find that your letter "matches" one of these letters in their database, your dispute will most likely be flagged as Frivolous, suspicious or it is simply ignored.

If you use poor or simplistic Credit Repair Software or Dispute Letters out of Credit Repair Books you might have firsthand experience with this.

No matter who writes the dispute letters or how threatening they are, if the scanned version DOES NOT match that of a "Boiler Plate" dispute letter used thousands of times, the scanned version will then be sent electronically overseas for processing. There, an outsource employee will look at the scanned dispute and assign a 3 digit code (even if it has Multiple pages of detailed documentation supporting the claim). Around 85% of disputes will fall under the same 5 codes.

E-Oscar Explained

e-OSCAR is a web-based, Metro 2 compliant, automated system that enables Data Furnishers (Credit Issuers like Bank of America Visa Credit Card and Collection Agencies like NCO Financial), and Credit Reporting Agencies (CRAs) to create and respond to consumer credit history disputes (the Dispute Letters that you mail to them).

Credit Reporting Agencies (CRAs) include Equifax, Experian, Innovis and TransUnion, their affiliates or Independent Credit Bureaus and Mortgage Reporting Companies. e-OSCAR also provides for Data Furnishers (DFs) to send "out-of-cycle" credit history updates to Credit Reporting Agencies (Equifax, Experian, Innovis and TransUnion).

The system primarily supports Automated Credit Dispute Verification (ACDV) and Automated Universal Data form (AUD) processing as well as a number of related processes that handle registration, subscriber code management and reporting. This system was created to reduce the overhead caused by about 20 thousand dispute letters received by the CRAs every day.

Credit Repair is very specialized in many situations. If you need personal guidance on a specific issue you can call me. My phone number and information is on **PAGE 156.**
My Experience: Finance Degree, 6 years loans officer at a national bank, 4 1/2 years credit bureau manager for one of the big three credit bureau's   John D. Harris

Thru the e-OSCAR system, the dispute processor reads the dispute and classifies it under a dispute code selected from a menu. Of these dispute codes, 85% of disputes fall under the same 5 codes. As you can see in the following chart, more than 50% of the disputes are grouped under the classifications of "Not mine and Account Status" which seem to be the more common mistakes incurred by Credit Reporting Agencies.

E-Oscar Codes

001 Not his/hers.
002 Belongs to another individual with same/similar name.
006 Not aware of collection.
008 Late due to change of address & never received statement.
010 Settlement or partial payments accepted.
012 Claims paid the original creditor before collection status or paid before charge-off.
014 Claims paid before collection status.
019 Included in the bankruptcy of another person.
023 Claims account closed.
024 Claims account closed by consumer.
031 Contract cancelled or rescinded.
037 Account included in bankruptcy.
038 Claims active military duty.
039 Insurance claim delayed.
040 Account involved in litigation.
041 Claims victim of natural or declared disaster.
100 Claims account deferred.
101 Not liable for account (i.e., ex-spouse, business).
102 Account reaffirmed or not included in bankruptcy.
103 Claims true identity fraud/account fraudulently opened.
104 Claims account take-over, fraudulent charges made on account.
105 Disputes Dates of Last Payment/Opened/of First Delinquency/Billing/Closed.
106 Disputes present/previous Account Status/Payment History Profile/ Payment Rating.
107 Disputes Special Comment/Compliance Condition Code/narrative remarks.
108 Disputes Account Type or Terms Duration/Terms Frequency or Portfolio Type disputed.
109 Disputes current balance.
110 Claims company will change.
111 Claims company will delete.
112 Claims inaccurate information.

Thru the e-OSCAR system, the dispute processor reads the dispute and classifies it under a dispute code selected from a menu. Of these dispute codes, 85% of disputes fall under the same 5 codes. As you can see in the following chart, more than 50% of the disputes are grouped under the classifications of "Not mine and Account Status" which seem to be the more common mistakes incurred by Credit Reporting Agencies.

Reasons of Dispute Percentages

Reason of Dispute	% of Disputes
Not Mine	31%
Account Status	21%
Inaccurate Information	17%
Account Amounts	9%
Account Closed	7%
Disputes Fall Under Same 5 Codes:	**85%**

Once your dispute is converted to one of the "Standardized Dispute Codes" within the e-OSCAR system, the code is sent via e-OSCAR to the Data Furnisher (the Original Creditor or Collection Agency) using a standardized form known as an Automated Credit Dispute Verification Form (ACDV).

When the data furnisher receives an ACDV thru the e-OSCAR system they should begin an "in-depth" investigation. If the furnisher is a Collection Agency, they should contact the Original Creditor for real documentation on the account, but the data furnisher will never receive nor see all the documentation part of the dispute.

Data Furnishers can receive thousands of disputes a month. e-OSCAR's solution to the problem is to send the Data Furnisher all these disputes in one large file (batch file), all at one time. When the data furnisher receives this file, there are several options for processing the data. One such option is called reply all.

This option allows the data furnisher to select a response like "Account Verified" and apply this response to multiple records in the file with a single click.

Another function called "Auto-Populate" allows the data furnisher to Auto Populate responses of ACDV before submitting them back to the credit bureau via the e-OSCAR system.

Credit Repair is very specialized in many situations. If you need personal guidance on a specific issue you can call me. My phone number and information is on **PAGE 156.**

My Experience: Finance Degree, 6 years loans officer at a national bank, 4 1/2 years credit bureau manager for one of the big three credit bureau's   John D. Harris

What is Rapid Rescoring

Say you applied for a mortgage but your credit score was just a few points shy of landing best possible interest rate due to an error on your credit report or a high balance. If you tried to fix the error or paid down the balance, it could take several weeks for your credit report to be updated through the normal channels.

Thanks to a process called rapid rescoring, you could potentially get approved for a mortgage at the lower interest rate within a few days.

If I paid off a credit card today, it might show up on my credit report 6-8 weeks from today.

Rapid rescore is simply a matter of providing documentation to the credit bureaus to get them to update information and shorten the normal reporting timetable. An updated score is typically generated within about 72 hours.

Loan originators look at your credit reports and scores from Equifax, Experian, and TransUnion, then base your eligibility and interest rate on your middle score, ignoring the high and low scores. That means you'd only need to have the median score recalculated instead of recalculating all three.

If your middle scores aren't good enough, your lender or mortgage broker is going to have a hard time getting you qualified for a loan or getting you qualified at the best terms. And since mortgage lenders are largely compensated on a commission basis, it's in their best interest to get you qualified. Plus, they are probably very familiar with what affects credit score.

So, at this point the goal becomes to get your credit reports modified, corrected, or updated so that your credit scores will improve enough to get you qualified.

Before going through the rapid rescore process, a loan officer could run a FICO simulator to estimate how much your credit score could be improved by paying down a balance or making other changes.

The impact of a rapid rescore varies depending on what derogatory items were on your credit report, it could save you thousands of dollars in interest over the course of a loan.

Nowadays, you can access credit score simulator on FICO.com and other websites. It is critical to understand some of them are based on vantage credit score developed by the 3 credit bureaus and some are based on FICO score.

It simulates scenarios of changing the values of credit factors, such as late payments, high credit limit and more credit cards. Then the decision tree will guide you through a list of qualification questions and spin out a hypothetical score.

Be aware that, the score is not guaranteed. However, credit simulator is a good tool to understand the impact and find a path to improve your credit scores.

However, it's important to note that a rapid rescore is different from credit repair.

With a rapid rescore, you'd need documentation that you'd actually paid off a high balance or collections or that an item on your credit report was reported inaccurately.

Unless your median credit score already tops 740 (the cut-off credit score for the best interest rates), it's probably in your best interest to consider a rapid rescore. "That low score is increasing the cost of the mortgage dramatically.

The process many mortgage lenders use is called rapid rescoring or rapid updating. It's the process whereby they are able to get information on your credit reports changed much faster than if you were to attempt to get it changed on your own. And, since credit-scoring systems are real-time, meaning your scores will change as your credit reports change, any positive modifications can mean better scores immediately.

Normally, credit reports take up to 45 days to "correct" if the consumer were to go through the standard protocol of filing disputes with the credit reporting agencies. In the case of a mortgage loan application, 45 days just isn't good enough because you could lose your interest rate lock. Enter rapid rescoring, the fee-based service offered by the companies who sell credit reports to your mortgage lenders.

For between $25-$50 per account per credit report (a cost absorbed by your mortgage lender), your mortgage lender can actually have information changed/updated on your credit reports within a few days rather than few weeks. They accomplish this by having atypical access to a specialized team of people at the credit reporting agencies that work directly with members of the mortgage industry to facilitate these expedited credit report corrections. For example, if you have a credit card incorrectly showing a $1,000 balance (that's actually paid off), your lender can have the credit report updated to show a $0 balance faster than you can say "wow, now that was fast."

Once the process of updating your credit files is completed, the mortgage lender can simply order an updated set of credit reports.

When the credit reports are re-pulled from the credit reporting agencies, the applicant's FICO credit scores will take into account the fact that the credit card now has a $0 balance. And, in many cases this will result in a better set of scores and possibly an approval rather than a denial.

The impression is that the applicant's scores were rapidly changed, which isn't at all what happened. All that happened was the credit reports, which were not up to date in the first place, were corrected — thus yielding a more accurate set of credit scores. So, in a sense, rapid "re-scoring" is really little more than "rapid-correcting" of your credit files, and just one more tool when you are trying to figure out how to fix your credit.

Credit Repair is very specialized in many situations. If you need personal guidance on a specific issue you can call me. My phone number and information is on **PAGE 156.**
My Experience: Finance Degree, 6 years loans officer at a national bank, 4 1/2 years credit bureau manager for one of the big three credit bureau's   John D. Harris

Should You Claim Bankruptcy

Personally I love the bankruptcy option. You wipe out your debts and your credit repairs very quickly. Here is why. Your credit is a score of your ability to repay debt. If most of your debt has been wiped out you are credit worthy. I have seen it time and time again. Someone with a low score claims bankruptcy and in two years they have no debt and great credit. If bankruptcy works for you do it. Don't worry about the stigma associated with bankruptcy. Just do it. It is a rather simple process. Shop around for an affordable attorney that will take payments.

Bankruptcy is a scary proposition. The word "bankruptcy" itself sounds so ominous. The media bombards us with nightmare tales of seemingly solid business giants going from bedrock to bankrupt. The list of the bankrupt runs the spectrum from personal to corporate bringing together the likes of Donald Trump with Enron.

And gossip columns never tire of dishing on the latest celebrity inches from bankruptcy whether it's Gary Coleman or Mike Tyson having to part with his pet tigers. You might even fear that you're a few steps from going under. After all, we live in an economy in which credit card offers clutter our mailboxes. And living in debt is an accepted norm. But, just how can you tell when it's time to throw in the towel and declare bankruptcy?

Here are a few questions to help you assess your financial danger zone:

Do you only make minimum payments on your credit cards?
Are bill collectors calling you?
Does the thought of sorting out your finances make you feel scared or out of control?
Do you use credit cards to pay for necessities?
Are you considering debt consolidation?
Are you unsure how much you actually owe?
Assess Your Situation

If you answered yes to two or more of the questions above, you at least want to give your financial situation a little more thought. Simply put, bankruptcy is when you owe more than you can afford to pay.

To determine where you are financially, inventory all of your liquid assets. Don't forget to include retirement funds, stocks, bonds, real estate, vehicles, college savings accounts, and other non-bank account funds. Add up a rough estimate for each item.

Then, collect and add up your bills and credit statements. If the value of your assets is less than the amount of debt you owe, declaring bankruptcy may be one way out of a sticky financial situation. However, bankruptcy shouldn't be approached casually. After all, it's not a simple, easy cure-all for out-of-control debt.

How Do You Claim Bankruptcy

You can go bankrupt in one of two main ways. The more common route is to voluntarily file for bankruptcy. The second way is for creditors to ask the court to order a person bankrupt.

There are several ways to file bankruptcy, each with pros and cons. You may want to consult a lawyer before proceeding so you can figure out the best fit for your circumstances.

Chapter 7 Bankruptcy

There are lots of reasons people file for Chapter 7 bankruptcy. You're probably not the only one, whatever your reason is. Some common reasons for filing for bankruptcy are unemployment, large medical expenses, seriously overextended credit, and marital problems. Chapter 7 is sometimes referred to as a "straight bankruptcy." A Chapter 7 bankruptcy liquidates your assets to pay off as much of your debt as possible. The cash from your assets is distributed to creditors like banks and credit card companies.

Within four months, you will receive a notice of discharge. The record of your bankruptcy will stay on your credit report for ten years. But even that doesn't have to mean doom. Lots of Chapter 7 filers have bought homes with recent bankruptcies on their record. For many people, Chapter 7 offers a quick, fresh start.

But Chapter 7 bankruptcies aren't right for everyone. Almost all assets are taken and sold to repay creditors. If a debtor owns a company, a family home, or any other personal assets which he or she wants to keep, Chapter 7 may not be the best option.

Chapter 13 Bankruptcy

For people who have property they want to keep, filing a Chapter 13 bankruptcy may be the better choice.

A Chapter 13 bankruptcy is also known as a reorganization bankruptcy. Chapter13 enables people to pay off their debts over a period of three to five years. For individuals who have consistent, predictable annual income, Chapter 13 offers a grace period. Any debts remaining at the end of the grace period are discharged.

Once the bankruptcy is approved by the court, creditors must stop contacting the

Credit Repair is very specialized in many situations. If you need personal guidance on a specific issue you can call me. My phone number and information is on **PAGE 156.**
My Experience: Finance Degree, 6 years loans officer at a national bank, 4 1/2 years credit bureau manager for one of the big three credit bureau's   John D. Harris

debtor. Bankrupt individuals may then continue working and paying off their debts over the coming years, and still keep their property and possessions.

Declaring Bankruptcy: Scary, But Sometimes Necessary

It can be hard to admit you need help getting out of debt, or that you can't do it alone. But that's why our government has bankruptcy laws to protect not only the creditors, but you! If you have a nerve-racking debt-load, it may be time to face financial facts. Perhaps you've been trying to ignore the ringing phone and the pile of unpaid bills that won't go away.

However, you could be doing yourself a disservice by not filing for bankruptcy. With a good lawyer and the right information, filing bankruptcy could give you the financial footing you need to get a fresh start. In other words, throwing in the towel may just be the beginning you need.

What Can You Dismiss in a Bankruptcy

Credit cards or unsecured loans.

Car repossessions and deficiency's
Some car accidents.
Material supplier debts.
Medical bills.
Lawsuits and judgments.
Evictions and unpaid rent.
Unpaid utility bills.
Foreclosure balances

What Can't You Dismiss in Bankruptcy

Taxes and tax liens
Student loans
Alimony and child support
Debts obtained through fraud
Debts you failed to schedule in time to allow creditors to file proofs of claim (unscheduled debts)
Debts for fraud while you were acting in a fiduciary capacity, or for embezzlement or larceny
Debts for willful and malicious injury
Debts for fines or penalties to governmental units
Debts for judgments in wrongful death or personal injury lawsuits resulting from motor

vehicle, vessel or aircraft accidents while you were intoxicated
Condominium or cooperative association fees or assessments

However, you could be doing yourself a disservice by not filing for bankruptcy. With a good lawyer and the right information, filing bankruptcy could give you the financial footing you need to get a fresh start. In other words, throwing in the towel may just be the beginning you need.

How Will Bankruptcy Effect Your Credit

The main issue that discourages most people from filing bankruptcy is the detrimental effect is has on their credit. It's true that a bankruptcy can stay on your credit report for up to ten years and it seriously hurts your credit score. However, not filing for bankruptcy and allowing your debts to go to collections will also negatively impact your credit.

Depending on the kind of bankruptcy you file, Chapter 7 vs Chapter 13 bankruptcy, your credit score will decrease anywhere from 160 to 220 points. This is enough to take a good credit rating down to a fair or poor one. Since most lenders decide whether or not to extend you credit based on your credit score, a bankruptcy will make it much more difficult to qualify for an auto or home loan or credit cards.

The primary remedy for this is time, though there are additional measures you can take to positively enhance your credit report and score. Ultimately, if you manage your new debts well, your score will gradually increase, and in time you will be able to run your financial life successfully, even if the bankruptcy has not yet dropped off your report.

How Long Will Bankruptcy Effect Your Credit

The bankruptcy itself and the debts associated with the bankruptcy will be displayed differently on your credit report. A completed Chapter 13 bankruptcy will stay on your report for up to seven years, and discharged debts will also stay on the report up to seven years after they are discharged. Since many debts will remain active in a Chapter 13 bankruptcy until the end of a three to five year payment plan, the debts that were discharged could actually remain on the report longer than the bankruptcy itself.

A completed Chapter 7 bankruptcy will stay on your credit report for up to ten years. Moreover, because all debts associated with a Chapter 7 bankruptcy are discharged within a few months of filing, they should drop off the report a few years before the bankruptcy itself. In general, discharged debt drops off a credit report after 7 years.

Basically, as the items on your report associated with the bankruptcy get older, they will have less and less of an effect on your credit score. This, by the way, may speak to the timeliness of filing for bankruptcy as opposed to letting collections accounts linger and then filing later.

Credit Repair is very specialized in many situations. If you need personal guidance on a specific issue you can call me. My phone number and information is on **PAGE 156.**

My Experience: Finance Degree, 6 years loans officer at a national bank, 4 1/2 years credit bureau manager for one of the big three credit bureau's   John D. Harris

Don't Consulate Debts

I personally hate these debt consultation companies,   DO NOT USE THEM.   IT DOESN'T WORK.

Myth: Debt consolidation saves interest, and you have one smaller payment.

Truth: Debt consolidation is dangerous because you treat only the symptom.

Debt consolidation is nothing more than a "con" because you think you've done something about the debt problem. The debt is still there, as are the habits that caused it — you just moved it! You can't borrow your way out of debt. You can't get out of a hole by digging out the bottom. True debt help is not quick or easy.

A friend of mine works for a debt consolidation firm whose internal statistics estimate that 78% of the time, after someone consolidates his credit card debt, the debt grows back. Why? He still doesn't have a game plan to either pay cash or not buy at all. He also hasn't saved for "unexpected events" which will also become debt.

Debt consolidation seems appealing because there is a lower interest rate on some of the debt and a lower payment. However, in almost every case we review, we find that the lower payment exists not because the rate is actually lower but because the term is extended. If you stay in debt longer, you get a lower payment, but if you stay in debt longer, you pay the lender more, which is why they are in the debt consolidation business.

Debt Consolidation Example
For example, let's say you have $30,000 in unsecured debt, including a two-year loan for $10,000 at 12%, and a four-year loan for $20,000 at 10%. Your monthly payment on the $10,000 loan is $517 and $583 on the $20,000 loan, for a total payment of $1,100 per month. The debt consolidation company tells you they have been able to lower your payment to $640 per month and your interest rate to 9% by negotiating with your creditors and rolling the loans together into one. Sounds great, doesn't it? Who wouldn't want to pay $460 less per month in payments?

But they don't tell you that it will now take you six years to pay off the loan. This may not sound that bad to you at first unless you realize how much more you will actually pay in additional payments. You will now pay $46,080 to pay off the new loan vs. $40,392 for the original loans, even with the lower interest rate of 9%. This means you paid $5,688 more for the "lower payment." Not such a good deal after all. This example shows you why they are in the business — because they make money off of you.

Attacking the Axis

Get Your Spies (Credit Monitoring)

Remember this is a war.

You can get a copy of all three reports here but

DON'T GET YOUR REPORTS HERE

www.annualcreditreport.com

If you use this site credit bureaus have 45 instead of 30 days to respond.

You need this time line to your advantage.

NEVER USE ANNUALCREDITREPORT.COM

So AGAIN NEVER USE THIS SITE

www.annualcreditreport.com

Credit Repair is very specialized in many situations. If you need personal guidance on a specific issue you can call me. My phone number and information is on **PAGE 156.**
My Experience: Finance Degree, 6 years loans officer at a national bank, 4 1/2 years credit bureau manager for one of the big three credit bureau's   John D. Harris

What is Credit Monitoring

Credit monitoring is a service that acts like a watchdog over your credit file and notifies you of any major changes to it so you are quickly alerted to any fraud on your accounts. Because the activities of fraudsters opening accounts in your name will show up first on your credit report within 30 days, especially when they fail to make payments on fraudulent accounts in your name, credit monitoring is helpful in detecting fraud on your accounts. The problem with credit monitoring is that it only catches the thievery once your accounts have already been hacked or used fraudulently and so it cannot protect your accounts from fraud or hacking.

Keeping tabs on your credit accounts can also show you your progress when trying to repair or build your credit, so credit monitoring is also very helpful in knowing where your credit stands

You need to monitor your credit so you can see your progress with credit repair.

Now remember you have 3 FICO Scores

Monitoring TransUnion and Equifax

Here are the two spy's you need. Now you will be able to monitor what all three of your scores are doing in real time. This is an absolute must.

You can access your Trans Union and Equifax. FICO score for free on

www.CreditKarma.com.

They use the Calculation using the Vantage Score 3.0 model, these scores range from 300 to 850

Why Use CreditKarma.com

Credit Karma is always 100% free.

What's the Catch?

You may be wondering, "If Credit Karma is really free, how do they make money? Do they sell my information?" No. Rest assured, they don't make money by selling your information. It's against their privacy policy

Are going to be bombarded with ads?" Simply put, they do generate revenue through advertising partners, but it may not be the kind of advertising you imagine. Rather, their goal is to provide personalized offers that might be helpful to you based on your current credit situation.

Credit Karma recommendations are based on powerful algorithms that find products based on your credit profile. These offers may include refinancing options if you look like you might be overpaying for a loan, or credit cards that could help you optimize your savings and earnings (just to name a few).

You are never under any obligation to take their offers.

Do yourself a favor and sign up today.

Monitoring Experian

You can access your Experian report and score here.

http://www.experian.com/

Introductory price of $4.95 for your first month of access, then just $19.95 each additional month. Cancel anytime if not satisfied.

Credit score calculated based on FICO® Score 8 model.

Score 8, are designed to predict the ... versions range from 250-900 (compared to 300-850 for base FICO® Scores

Keep this service until your credit is cleaned up.

Please Note Industry Scores

Experian
Regular-FICO® Score 8
Auto Lending- FICO® Auto Score 8
Credit Cards- FICO® Bankcard Score 8
Mortgage- FICO® Score 2

Equifax
Regular-FICO® Score 8
Auto Lending- FICO® Auto Score 8
Credit Cards- FICO® Bankcard Score 8
Mortgage- FICO® Score 5

TransUnion
Regular-FICO® Score 8
Auto Lending- FICO® Auto Score 8
Credit Cards- FICO® Bankcard Score 8
Mortgage- FICO® Score 4

SPY'S CAN BE TRAITORS

All three major credit bureaus have arbitration agreements in their terms of use,

That means if you buy your credit report online and find an error on it, you can still dispute the error. However, if you disagree with how the credit bureau managed the dispute and want to take the bureau to court, the credit bureau can legally press the arbitration clause and force you to give up your right to argue your case before a jury.

That can make it much more difficult to prove your case and win substantial damages if you've been financially wronged, say consumer lawyers.

In arbitration, your complaint will be handled by an individual arbitrator, appointed from an arbitration association chosen by the credit bureau, and it will be solely up to the arbitrator to decide your case. If you disagree with the arbitrator's decision, you are not allowed to appeal.

Forced arbitration clauses never help the consumer.

They only help the business that does something wrong.

You NEED TO mail an opt-out letter to the credit bureau's within 30 to 60 days of receiving the report.

TransUnion's Forced Arbitration Terms of Service

HERE IS THE ONE TRANSUNION SNEAKES INTO THEIR TERMS OF USE:

AGREEMENT TO RESOLVE DISPUTES BY BINDING INDIVIDUAL ARBITRATION

THIS SECTION IS AN AGREEMENT TO ARBITRATE DISPUTES ("ARBITRATION AGREEMENT") THAT MAY ARISE AS A RESULT OF YOUR TRANSUNION INTERACTIVE MEMBERSHIPS, PRODUCTS OR SERVICES OR THE AGREEMENT. READ THIS SECTION CAREFULLY. YOU UNDERSTAND AND AGREE THAT BOTH PARTIES WOULD HAVE HAD A RIGHT TO LITIGATE DISPUTES THROUGH A COURT AND TO HAVE A JUDGE OR JURY DECIDE THEIR CASE, BUT BOTH PARTIES BY ENTERING INTO THIS AGREEMENT CHOOSE TO HAVE ANY DISPUTE RESOLVED THROUGH BINDING INDIVIDUAL ARBITRATION. OTHER RIGHTS THAT YOU WOULD HAVE IF YOU WENT TO COURT MAY NOT BE AVAILABLE OR MAY BE MORE LIMITED IN ARBITRATION, INCLUDING YOUR RIGHT TO APPEAL.

RIGHT TO REJECT ARBITRATION

YOU HAVE THE RIGHT TO REJECT THIS ARBITRATION AGREEMENT, BUT YOU MUST EXERCISE THIS RIGHT PROMPTLY. You must notify us in writing within sixty (60) days after the date you click-on to "Accept" the Agreement. You must send your request to: TransUnion Interactive, 100 Cross Street, Suite 202, San Luis Obispo, CA 93401. This request must include your current username and a clear statement of your intent, such as "I reject the arbitration clause in the TransUnion Interactive Service Agreement."

Credit Repair is very specialized in many situations. If you need personal guidance on a specific issue you can call me. My phone number and information is on **PAGE 156.**

My Experience: Finance Degree, 6 years loans officer at a national bank, 4 1/2 years credit bureau manager for one of the big three credit bureau's   John D. Harris

Equifax's Forced Arbitration Terms of Service

HERE IS THE ONE EQUIFAX SNEAKES INTO THEIR TERMS OF USE:

AGREEMENT TO RESOLVE ALL DISPUTES BY BINDING INDIVIDUAL ARBITRATION. PLEASE READ THIS ENTIRE SECTION CAREFULLY BECAUSE IT AFFECTS YOUR LEGAL RIGHTS. THIS SECTION PROVIDES THAT EXCEPT AS PROVIDED BELOW, ANY AND ALL CLAIMS OR DISPUTES BETWEEN YOU AND US WILL BE RESOLVED BY BINDING ARBITRATION BEFORE A NEUTRAL ARBITRATOR THAT REPLACES THE RIGHT TO GO TO COURT AND MAY LIMIT YOUR RIGHTS TO DISCOVERY OR TO APPEAL. IT FURTHER PROVIDES THAT YOU WILL NOT BE ABLE TO BRING A CLASS ACTION OR OTHER REPRESENTATIVE ACTION IN COURT, NOR WILL YOU BE ABLE TO BRING ANY CLAIM IN ARBITRATION AS A CLASS ACTION OR OTHER REPRESENTATIVE ACTION. YOU WILL NOT BE ABLE TO BE PART OF ANY CLASS ACTION OR OTHER REPRESENTATIVE ACTION BROUGHT BY ANYONE ELSE.

Binding Arbitration. Either You or Equifax may, without the other's consent, elect mandatory, binding arbitration of any Claim (as defined below) raised by either You or Equifax against the other. As used in this arbitration provision, the term "Claim" or "Claims" means any claim, dispute, or controversy between You and Us regarding any aspect of Your relationship with Equifax, including but not limited to any Claim arising from these Terms of Use or arising from Your use of the Products or this Site or any information You receive from Us, whether based on contract, statute, common law, regulation, ordinance, tort, or any other legal or equitable theory regardless of what remedy is sought. Additionally, for purposes of this arbitration provision "Equifax" or "Us" will include Equifax's Suppliers, parents, subsidiaries, affiliates, successors, assigns, employees, agents, and any third party providing products, services, or benefits in connection with a Product provided to You. The term "Claim" shall have the broadest possible construction. If You or We elect arbitration, the arbitration will be conducted as an individual arbitration. Neither You nor We consent or agree to any arbitration on a class or representative basis, and the arbitrator shall have no authority to proceed with arbitration on a class or representative basis. No arbitration will be consolidated with any other arbitration proceeding without the consent of all parties. This arbitration provision applies to and includes any Claims made and remedies sought as part of any class action, private attorney general action, or other representative action. By consenting to submit Your Claims to arbitration, You will be forfeiting Your right to share in any class action awards, including class claims where a class has not yet been certified, even if the facts and circumstances upon which the Claims are based already occurred or existed. As an exception to the arbitration provision, You retain the right to pursue in small claims court any Claim that is within that court's jurisdiction and proceed on an individual basis.
Right to Opt-Out of this Arbitration Provision. IF YOU DO NOT WISH TO BE BOUND BY THE ARBITRATION PROVISION, YOU HAVE THE RIGHT TO EXCLUDE YOURSELF. Opting out of the arbitration provision will have no adverse effect on your relationship with Equifax or the delivery of Products to You by Equifax. In order to exclude Yourself from the arbitration provision, You must notify Equifax in writing within 30 days of the date that You first accept these Terms of Use on the Site (for Products purchased from Equifax on the Site). If You purchased Your Product other than on the Site, and thus these Terms of Use were mailed, emailed or otherwise delivered to You, then You must notify Equifax in writing

within 30 days of the date that You receive the Terms of Use. You may opt-out by writing to Equifax Consumer Services LLC, Attn.: Arbitration Opt-Out, P.O. Box 105496, Atlanta, GA 30348. Your written notification to Equifax must include Your name, address, and Equifax User ID, as well as a clear statement that You do not wish to resolve disputes with Equifax through arbitration.

Credit Repair is very specialized in many situations. If you need personal guidance on a specific issue you can call me. My phone number and information is on **PAGE 156.**

My Experience: Finance Degree, 6 years loans officer at a national bank, 4 1/2 years credit bureau manager for one of the big three credit bureau's   John D. Harris

Experian's Forced Arbitration Terms of Service

HERE IS THE ONE EXPERIAN SNEAKES INTO THEIR TERMS OF USE:

DISPUTE RESOLUTION BY BINDING ARBITRATION
PLEASE READ THIS CAREFULLY. IT AFFECTS YOUR RIGHTS.

SUMMARY:
MOST CUSTOMER CONCERNS CAN BE RESOLVED QUICKLY AND TO THE CUSTOMER'S SATISFACTION BY CALLING CIC'S CUSTOMER SERVICE DEPARTMENT AT 1-877-284-7942. IN THE UNLIKELY EVENT THAT CIC'S CUSTOMER SERVICE DEPARTMENT IS UNABLE TO RESOLVE A COMPLAINT YOU MAY HAVE REGARDING THE SERVICE, SERVICE WEBSITE, OR ITS CONTENT TO YOUR SATISFACTION (OR IF CIC HAS NOT BEEN ABLE TO RESOLVE A DISPUTE IT HAS WITH YOU AFTER ATTEMPTING TO DO SO INFORMALLY), WE EACH AGREE TO RESOLVE THOSE DISPUTES THROUGH BINDING ARBITRATION OR SMALL CLAIMS COURT INSTEAD OF IN COURTS OF GENERAL JURISDICTION TO THE FULLEST EXTENT PERMITTED BY LAW. ARBITRATION IS MORE INFORMAL THAN A LAWSUIT IN COURT. ARBITRATION USES A NEUTRAL ARBITRATOR INSTEAD OF A JUDGE OR JURY, ALLOWS FOR MORE LIMITED DISCOVERY THAN IN COURT, AND IS SUBJECT TO VERY LIMITED REVIEW BY COURTS. ARBITRATORS CAN AWARD THE SAME DAMAGES AND RELIEF THAT A COURT CAN AWARD. ANY ARBITRATION UNDER THIS AGREEMENT WILL TAKE PLACE ON AN INDIVIDUAL BASIS; CLASS ARBITRATIONS AND CLASS ACTIONS ARE NOT PERMITTED. CIC WILL PAY ALL COSTS OF ARBITRATION, NO MATTER WHO WINS, SO LONG AS YOUR CLAIM IS NOT FRIVOLOUS. HOWEVER, IN ARBITRATION, BOTH YOU AND CIC WILL BE ENTITLED TO RECOVER ATTORNEYS´ FEES FROM THE OTHER PARTY TO THE SAME EXTENT AS YOU WOULD BE IN COURT.

Arbitration Agreement:
(a) CIC and you agree to arbitrate all disputes and claims between us arising out of this Agreement directly related to the Service, Service Website, or its content, except any disputes or claims which under governing law are not subject to arbitration. This agreement to arbitrate is intended to be broadly interpreted and to make all disputes and claims between us directly relating to the provision of the Service, your use of the Service Website, or its content subject to arbitration to the fullest extent permitted by law. However, for the avoidance of doubt, any dispute you may have with us arising out of the Fair Credit Reporting Act ("FCRA") relating to the information contained in your consumer disclosure or report, including but not limited to claims for alleged inaccuracies, shall not be governed by this agreement to arbitrate. The agreement to arbitrate otherwise includes, but is not limited to:

claims arising out of or relating to any aspect of the relationship between us arising out of the Service, Service Website, or its content, whether based in contract, tort, statute (including, without limitation, the Credit Repair Organizations Act) fraud, misrepresentation or any other legal theory; claims that arose before this or any prior Agreement (including, but not limited to, claims relating to advertising); claims that are currently the subject of purported class action litigation in which you are not a member of a certified class; and claims that may arise after the termination of this Agreement.

For purposes of this arbitration provision, references to "CIC," "you," and "us" shall include our respective parent entities, subsidiaries, affiliates, agents, employees, predecessors in interest, successors and assigns, websites of the foregoing, as well as all authorized or unauthorized users or beneficiaries of services, products or information under this or prior Agreements between us relating to the Service, Service Website, or its content. Notwithstanding the foregoing, either party may bring an individual action in small claims court. You agree that, by entering into this Agreement, you and CIC are each waiving the right to a trial by jury or to participate in a class action. This Agreement evidences a transaction in interstate commerce, and thus the Federal Arbitration Act governs the interpretation and enforcement of this arbitration provision. This arbitration provision shall survive termination of this Agreement.

(b) A party who intends to seek arbitration must first send to the other, by certified mail, a written Notice of Dispute ("Notice"). The Notice to CIC should be addressed to: General Counsel, Experian, 475 Anton Boulevard, Costa Mesa, CA 92626 ("Notice Address"). The Notice must describe the nature and basis of the claim or dispute and set forth the specific relief you seek from CIC ("Demand"). If CIC and you do not reach an agreement to resolve the claim within 30 days after the Notice is received, you or CIC may commence an arbitration proceeding. During the arbitration, the amount of any settlement offer made by CIC or you shall not be disclosed to the arbitrator until after the arbitrator determines the amount, if any, to which you or CIC is entitled.

You may obtain more information about arbitration from www.adr.org.

(c) After CIC receives notice at the Notice Address that you have commenced arbitration, it will promptly reimburse you for your payment of the filing fee. (The filing fee currently is $200 for claims under $10,000, but is subject to change by the arbitration provider. If you are unable to pay this fee, CIC will pay it directly upon receiving a written request at the Notice Address.) The arbitration will be governed by the Commercial Dispute Resolution Procedures and the Supplementary Procedures for Consumer Related Disputes (collectively, "AAA Rules") of the American Arbitration Association ("AAA"), as modified by this Agreement, and will be administered by the AAA. If the AAA is unavailable or refuses to arbitrate the parties' dispute for any reason, the arbitration shall be administered and conducted by a widely-recognized arbitration organization that is mutually agreeable to the parties, but neither party shall unreasonably withhold their consent. If the parties cannot agree to a mutually agreeable arbitration organization, one shall be appointed pursuant to Section 5 of the Federal Arbitration Act. In all events, the AAA Rules shall govern the parties' dispute. The AAA Rules are available online at www.adr.org, by calling the AAA at 1-800-778-7879, or by writing to the Notice Address.

All issues are for the arbitrator to decide, including the scope and enforceability of this arbitration provision as well as the Agreement's other terms and conditions, and the arbitrator shall have exclusive authority to resolve any such dispute relating to the scope and enforceability of this arbitration provision or any other term of this Agreement including, but not limited to any claim that all or any part of this arbitration provision or Agreement is void or voidable. The arbitrator shall be bound by the terms of this Agreement. Unless CIC and you agree otherwise, any arbitration hearings will take place in the county (or parish) of your billing address. If your claim is for $10,000 or less, we agree that you may choose whether the arbitration will be conducted solely on the basis of documents submitted to the arbitrator, through a telephonic hearing, or by an in-person hearing as established by the AAA Rules. If your claim exceeds $10,000, the right to a hearing will be determined by the AAA Rules. Except as otherwise provided for herein, CIC will pay all AAA filing, administration and arbitrator fees for any arbitration initiated in accordance with the notice requirements above. If, however, the arbitrator finds that either the substance of your claim or the relief sought in the Demand is frivolous or brought for an improper purpose (as measured by the standards set forth in Federal Rule of Civil Procedure 11(b), then the payment of all such fees will be governed by the AAA Rules. In such case, you agree to

Credit Repair is very specialized in many situations. If you need personal guidance on a specific issue you can call me. My phone number and information is on **PAGE 156.**
My Experience: Finance Degree, 6 years loans officer at a national bank, 4 1/2 years credit bureau manager for one of the big three credit bureau's   John D. Harris

reimburse CIC for all monies previously disbursed by it that are otherwise your obligation to pay under the AAA Rules.

(d) The arbitrator may make rulings and resolve disputes as to the payment and reimbursement of fees and expenses at any time during the proceeding or in the final award, pursuant to applicable law and the AAA Rules.

(e) Discovery and/or the exchange of non-privileged information relevant to the dispute will be governed by the AAA Rules.

(f) YOU AND CIC AGREE THAT EACH MAY BRING CLAIMS AGAINST THE OTHER ONLY IN YOUR OR ITS INDIVIDUAL CAPACITY, AND NOT AS A PLAINTIFF OR CLASS MEMBER IN ANY PURPORTED CLASS OR REPRESENTATIVE PROCEEDING. Further, unless both you and CIC agree otherwise, the arbitrator may not consolidate more than one person's claims, and may not otherwise preside over any form of a representative or class proceeding. The arbitrator may award injunctive relief only in favor of the individual party seeking relief and only to the extent necessary to provide relief warranted by that party's individual claim. If this specific subparagraph (f) is found to be unenforceable, then the entirety of this arbitration provision shall be null and void.

(g) Notwithstanding any provision in this Agreement to the contrary, we agree that if CIC makes any change to this arbitration provision (other than a change to the Notice Address) during your membership in any credit monitoring or other product, you may reject any such change and require CIC to adhere to the language in this provision if a dispute between us arises regarding such membership product.

Opt Out of Forced Arbitration

Opt out now so you can go to jury if you have to. This also makes your threats to sue real.
If you threaten to sue but haven't sent in your Opt out letter you do not have that option.

Here's what you need to do:
Send the letter I provided to you
Enclose the Identification Form
Have it notarized
Send it registered mail
Keep copies and keep the mailing receipt

Credit Repair is very specialized in many situations. If you need personal guidance on a specific issue you can call me. My phone number and information is on **PAGE 156.**

My Experience: Finance Degree, 6 years loans officer at a national bank, 4 1/2 years credit bureau manager for one of the big three credit bureau's   John D. Harris

Identification Form

On the bottom of this   "ID DOCUMENT"

I declare under penalty of perjury (under the laws of the United States of America) that this identification provide is me
John Doe
Signature
Date

Opt Out Letter

Your Name
Address

Credit Repair is very specialized in many situations. If you need personal guidance on a specific issue you can call me. My phone number and information is on **PAGE 156**.

My Experience: Finance Degree, 6 years loans officer at a national bank, 4 1/2 years credit bureau manager for one of the big three credit bureau's   John D. Harris

City, State
Zip
SSN: 000-00-0000 | DOB: 1/1/1970
User ID:
(This is your user Id for your TransUnion or Equifax or Experian account)

CREDIT REPORTING AGENCY
PO BOX ADDRESS
CITY, STATE
ZIP CODE

I have recently purchase a credit report from (TransUnion Equifax Experian) Please use this written letter as confirmation that I hereby Opt out and do not wish to resolve disputes with Equifax through arbitration.

Again: I reject the arbitration clause in the TransUnion Interactive Service Agreement.

Thank you for noting my account.

{YOUR NAME HERE}
Signature:_____
Date: _____

IN WITNESS WHEREOF, the said party has signed and sealed these presents the day and year first above written. Signed, sealed and delivered in the presence of:
{PRINT YOUR NAME HERE} _____ Signature
STATE OF
COUNTY OF
I HEREBY CERTIFY that on this day before me, an officer duly qualified to take acknowledgments, personally appeared
{   YOUR   NAME   HERE   },   who   has   produced
_____ as   identification   and   who executed the foregoing instrument and he/she acknowledged before me that he/she executed the same.
WITNESS my hand and official seal in the County and State aforesaid this _____ day of _____2016.

_____ Notary Public
Printed Name
My commission expires:

---------------------End of Letter.

Now Get it Notarized

Now you need to get the letter(s) notarized.   You will add a copy of your social security card and Driver License (or passport) for proof of your identity and go a notary of the public. DO NOT SIGN THE LETTERS UNTIL YOU GO TO THE NOTARY AND THEY TELL YOU TO SIGN IT.

Opt Out Addresses

You may opt-out by writing to

Experian Consumer Services

Credit Repair is very specialized in many situations. If you need personal guidance on a specific issue you can call me. My phone number and information is on **PAGE 156.**
My Experience: Finance Degree, 6 years loans officer at a national bank, 4 1/2 years credit bureau manager for one of the big three credit bureau's   John D. Harris

Attn.: Arbitration Opt-Out
475 Anton Boulevard,
 Costa Mesa, CA 92626

Equifax Consumer Services LLC,
Attn.: Arbitration Opt-Out,
P.O. Box 105496,
Atlanta, GA 30348

TransUnion Interactive
Attn.: Arbitration Opt-Out,
100 Cross Street, Suite 202,
San Luis Obispo, CA 93401.

Now Track Your letters

Now your letters are ready to send. You will send your letter WITH TRACKING Priority Mail. This is your proof that CRA's get your letter(s).

This is an absolute must.

File all your paperwork.

Reading Your Reports

Now let's log into your creditkarma.com account. Here is what your will see.

Report Date: Feb 10, 2016

Provided by **TransUnion**

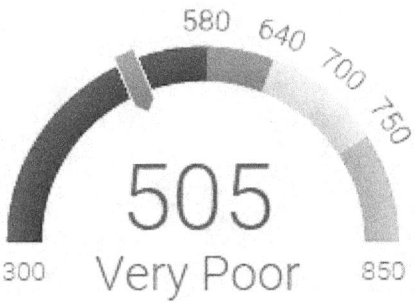

505
300 Very Poor 850

Go to **TransUnion** credit report

Report Date: Feb 10, 2016

Provided by **EQUIFAX**

540
300 Very Poor 850

Go to **Equifax** credit report

Now let's click on your TransUnion credit report

Credit Repair is very specialized in many situations. If you need personal guidance on a specific issue you can call me. My phone number and information is on **PAGE 156.**
My Experience: Finance Degree, 6 years loans officer at a national bank, 4 1/2 years credit bureau manager for one of the big three credit bureau's   John D. Harris

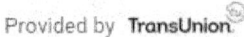

Provided by TransUnion

580   640   700   750

505
300   Very Poor   850

Go to **TransUnion** credit report

Now Lets Click on Your TransUnion Credit Report

Breakdown of Your Reports

Account Mix	8
Real Estate	6
Auto	1
Student	0
Other Loans	1
Total Accounts	16

Now obviously your report is going to look different but here is the breakdown of accounts.

Now Click on ACCOUNTS

Credit Repair is very specialized in many situations. If you need personal guidance on a specific issue you can call me. My phone number and information is on **PAGE 156.**
My Experience: Finance Degree, 6 years loans officer at a national bank, 4 1/2 years credit bureau manager for one of the big three credit bureau's   John D. Harris

Sample Accounts

Account Name
Account Type

Open Date

Status

Balance

ACCRED HOME

Mortgage

Nov 23, 2004

Closed

No Missed Payments

$0

AMC MTG SVCS

Mortgage

Nov 08, 2005

Closed

No Missed Payments

$0

AURORA BANK

Mortgage

Jul 19, 2006

Closed

$0

BK OF AMER

Credit Card

Nov 02, 2001

Closed

$7,808

BK OF AMER

Credit Card

Jun 01, 2007

Closed

No Missed Payments

$0

BK OF AMER

Credit Card

Feb 26, 2007

Closed

$38,331

BK OF AMER

Credit Card

Oct 19, 2001

Closed

$7,481

Credit Repair is very specialized in many situations. If you need personal guidance on a specific issue you can call me. My phone number and information is on **PAGE 156.**
My Experience: Finance Degree, 6 years loans officer at a national bank, 4 1/2 years credit bureau manager for one of the big three credit bureau's   John D. Harris

Specific Account Example 1

Now click on a specific account:

Account Details

Last Reported

Jun 02, 2006

Creditor Name

ACCRED HOME

Account Type

Conventional Real Estate Mortgage

Account Status

Closed

Opened Date

Nov 23, 2004

Closed Date

Jun 02, 2006

Limit

--

Term

360 Months

Monthly Payment

$3,810

Responsibility

Individual

Balance

$0

Highest Balance

$572,000

Payment Status

Current

Worst Payment Status

70

Date of Last Payment

Current

May 10, 2006

Amount Past Due

$0

Times 30/60/90 Days Late

0/0/0

Remarks

Closed

Payment History

2006 `OK` `OK` `OK` `OK` `OK`

2005 `OK` `OK` `OK` `OK` `OK` `OK` `OK` `OK` `OK` `OK` `OK` `OK`

2004   `OK` `OK`

J F M A M J J A S O N D

Creditor Contact Details

ACCREDITED HOME LENDERS

16550 W BERNARDO D 1

SAN DIEGO, CA

92127

(877) 683-4466

Direct Dispute

Specific Account Example 2

Credit Repair is very specialized in many situations. If you need personal guidance on a specific issue you can call me. My phone number and information is on **PAGE 156.**
My Experience: Finance Degree, 6 years loans officer at a national bank, 4 1/2 years credit bureau manager for one of the big three credit bureau's   John D. Harris

Here is another example:

Account Details

Last Reported

Jan 16, 2016

Creditor Name

BK OF AMER

Account Type

Credit Card

Account Status

Closed - Derogatory

Opened Date

Nov 02, 2001

Closed Date

Jun 06, 2009

Limit

$6,500

Term

--

Monthly Payment

$0

Responsibility

Individual

Balance

$7,808

Highest Balance

$7,808

Payment Status

Collection/Charge-Off

Worst Payment Status

Unknown

Date of Last Payment

Mar 02, 2009

Amount Past Due

$1,633

Times 30/60/90 Days Late

0/0/0

Remarks

Charged off as bad debt

Dismissed

Payment History

No payment history has been reported by this creditor.

Credit Utilization*

120.12%

Creditor Contact Details

BANK OF AMERICA

PO BOX 982238

EL PASO, TX

79998

(800) 421-2110

Direct Dispute

Specific Account Example 3

Credit Repair is very specialized in many situations. If you need personal guidance on a specific issue you can call me. My phone number and information is on **PAGE 156.**
 My Experience: Finance Degree, 6 years loans officer at a national bank, 4 1/2 years credit bureau manager for one of the big three credit bureau's   John D. Harris

CMRE FINANCIAL SERVICES

MED1 02 MEDICAL PAYMENT DATA

Jul 17, 2014

Open

$472

Account Details

Last Reported

Nov 21, 2015

Collection Agency

CMRE FINANCIAL SERVICES

Original Creditor

MED1 02 MEDICAL PAYMENT DATA

Status

Open

Opened Date

Jul 17, 2014

Closed Date

--

Responsibility

Individual

Balance

$472

High Balance

$416

Remarks

Placed for collection

Creditor Contact Details

CMRE FINANCIAL SERVICES

3075 E IMPERIAL HW 200

BREA, CA

92821

(877) 572-7555

Understanding Your Accounts

Click on all your accounts. Read and understand them. This is your credit and you need to know this site better than you know your car.

Any changes to your credit will show up once reported on this site.

Study Study Study these accounts. Then Study some more.

Sample Collection Account 1

Credit Repair is very specialized in many situations. If you need personal guidance on a specific issue you can call me. My phone number and information is on **PAGE 156.**
My Experience: Finance Degree, 6 years loans officer at a national bank, 4 1/2 years credit bureau manager for one of the big three credit bureau's   John D. Harris

Now click on "Collections" if you have any. Here is a sample:

Agency

Original Creditor

Open Date
Status

Balance

CMRE FINANCIAL SERVICES

MED1 02 MEDICAL PAYMENT DATA

Jul 17, 2014

Open

$472

Account Details

Last Reported

Nov 21, 2015

Collection Agency

CMRE FINANCIAL SERVICES

Original Creditor

MED1 02 MEDICAL PAYMENT DATA

Status

Open

Opened Date

Jul 17, 2014

Closed Date

--

Responsibility

Individual

Balance

$472

High Balance

$416

Remarks

Placed for collection

Creditor Contact Details

CMRE FINANCIAL SERVICES

3075 E IMPERIAL HW 200

BREA, CA

92821

(877) 572-7555

Direct Dispute

Sample Collection Account 2

Agency

Original Creditor

Credit Repair is very specialized in many situations. If you need personal guidance on a specific issue you can call me. My phone number and information is on **PAGE 156.**

My Experience: Finance Degree, 6 years loans officer at a national bank, 4 1/2 years credit bureau manager for one of the big three credit bureau's   John D. Harris

Open Date
Status

Balance

ENHANCED RECOVERY CORP

AT T

Mar 09, 2015

Open

$59

Account Details

Last Reported

Apr 26, 2015

Collection Agency

ENHANCED RECOVERY CORP

Original Creditor

AT T

Status

Open

Opened Date

Mar 09, 2015

Closed Date

--

Responsibility

Individual Account.

Balance

$59

High Balance

$59

Public Records

There are only three types of public records that appear in a credit report, all of them related to debts.

Bankruptcy is the most obvious. It is a legal proceeding under which a person is provided relief from debts they are unable to pay. There are two primary forms of

78

bankruptcy, called "chapters," because they are defined by chapters in the bankruptcy law.

Under Chapter 13 bankruptcy, a person repays at least a portion of their debts. Chapter 13 bankruptcy will remain in the credit report for seven years from the filing date.

Under Chapter 7 bankruptcy, a person does not repay any of the debts included in the filing. Chapter 7 bankruptcy remains on the credit report for 10 years from the filing date.

Court records are updated periodically, and the status of the bankruptcy, for instance that it has been discharged, will be updated automatically in the credit report.

The second public record you may see in a credit report is a tax lien. This results most commonly from failure to pay your taxes. Uncle Sam is serious about getting his taxes paid.

An unpaid tax lien will remain on a credit report for up to 10 years from the filing date. A paid tax lien is deleted seven years from the date it is paid.

Civil judgments are the third type of public record included in credit reports. A civil judgment is simply a debt you owe through the courts as a result of a lawsuit. If you have been sued and lost, you will likely owe a civil judgment. Once paid, the entry will be updated to show that fact.

Contrary to popular myth, there aren't any other public records that appear in a person's credit report.

The information is collected and updated regularly from the courts either by a representative of the credit reporting companies or provided directly by the court to the national credit reporting companies.

Public Records Sample

Now click on "Public Records" if you have any.

Here is a sample:
Public Record

Date

Status

Amount

Bankruptcy

Jul 15, 2011

Dismissed

$0

Bankruptcy

Nov 23, 2009

Discharged

Specific Public Record

Credit Repair is very specialized in many situations. If you need personal guidance on a specific issue you can call me. My phone number and information is on **PAGE 156.**
My Experience: Finance Degree, 6 years loans officer at a national bank, 4 1/2 years credit bureau manager for one of the big three credit bureau's   John D. Harris

Now click on a specific one:

Public Record Details

Reference Number

912287

Date Filed

Aug 18, 2009

Date

Nov 23, 2009

Status

Discharged

Amount

$0

Classification

Bankruptcy

Responsibility

Individual

Asset Amount

$0

Contact Details

CALIFORNIA FEDERAL COURT

JACOB WEINBURGER U 325 WEST F ST

SAN DIEGO , CA 92101

(619) 557-5620

Direct Dispute

Direct Dispute

Ok now here are the categories you need to go through.

Accounts
Credit Inquiries
Collections
Public Records
Missed Payments in History

Ok you need to go through every inch of your credit report. Spend a few hours each day for the next 3 days looking at your report.

You need to know every inch of this report.

Repairing your Credit Supplies

Preparing for the war. Here are the tools you will need:

Credit Repair is very specialized in many situations. If you need personal guidance on a specific issue you can call me. My phone number and information is on **PAGE 156.**

My Experience: Finance Degree, 6 years loans officer at a national bank, 4 1/2 years credit bureau manager for one of the big three credit bureau's   John D. Harris

1)   Pen
2)   **9 Folders**
3)   **Paper**
4)   **Access to a Printer**
5)   **Access to reports in real time from creditkarma.com**
       and Experian.com
6)   **30 Copies of Your Identification Form (page 101)**

Now when we say credit repair we are really talking about increasing your Fico score because that is the only important part of your credit.

Credit Repair Simplified

Here are the things we want to focus on:

1)   Bankruptcy   Yes/No

2)   Decrease your Credit utilization – "the amount you have borrowed compared to your credit limit" –This is a key ratio.

3)   Add credit lines that report to the credit bureaus.

4)   Add your utility bills

5)   Add accounts to your reports that are in good standing.

6)   Removing Adverse Items that not are yours.

7)   Removing Adverse Items that are yours.

8)   Be able to monitor everything from our credit monitoring.

Step 1: Do you declare Bankruptcy and be done with the whole thing.

The Basics of Credit Card Debt and Bankruptcy

In an economy where housing problems dominate the headlines, high interest credit cards still remain one of the largest issues consumers face in their fight for financial health. It should come as no surprise to learn then, that credit card debt is still one of the primary reasons consumers are forced to file for bankruptcy. When a credit card account has been delinquent for more than 180 days, banks will charge off what is owed as "bad debt" and sell the account to a debt collector who will call, harass and even sue if the past due balances are high enough. Mounting pressure from debt collectors pushes many consumers through the front door of a bankruptcy office because chapter 7 protection is widely perceived as the fastest and best way to get out from under unmanageable credit card debt. While it is true that filing for bankruptcy can help discharge credit card bills, there are some basics that every consumer needs to know before relying on bankruptcy as a debt relief measure.

In this post we will give you the basics so that you can evaluate whether bankruptcy is a good solution to your credit card problems. Please also be sure to browse the related posts section of this page for additional information.

Credit Card Debt is Dischargeable in Bankruptcy.

That's the number one rule when it comes to unsecured debts like credit cards debts and medical bills, they are dischargeable in bankruptcy. When you file for bankruptcy, all of your unsecured debts are eliminated, meaning you do not legally owe these bills any longer. Credit card companies who choose to pursue you for old, discharged debts will do so in violation of the law and will be subject to sanctions by the bankruptcy court. Furthermore, unlike debts that are forgiven through private negotiation with a lender, there is no tax liability for debts that are discharged in bankruptcy.

Your Credit Reports Should Show ZERO Balances on Your Credit Cards After Bankruptcy.

This is an area where consumers get tripped up. After bankruptcy, The credit card companies are required to report discharged debt as having a ZERO balance. It is often necessary to check your credit report and confirm its accuracy after your case closes.

Fraud Will Prevent Credit Card Debt From Being Discharged

While the general rule is that credit card debt is easily eliminated by filing for bankruptcy, fraudulent activity can jeopardize your entire bankruptcy discharge. Using credit cards for luxury purchases prior to bankruptcy creates a presumption of fraud which can be difficult to overcome. Don't use credit cards after meeting with a bankruptcy attorney unless you've decided not to file. The bottom line is any use of credit cards with the intention of not paying the debt back is fraudulent. The bankruptcy code protects debtors who behave in good faith and punish debtors who to try to game the system. For more information see: Using Credit Cards Before Bankruptcy is a Big No No!

Can You Keep a Credit Card Out of Your Bankruptcy?

All debts including credit card debts, must be disclosed in your bankruptcy petition. This means that you cannot keep any credit card that has a balance "out of your bankruptcy", it must be disclosed and will be discharged along with the rest of your unsecured debts. Credit cards with zero balances do not create a debt obligation and are therefore not required to be disclosed in a bankruptcy filing. For more information see: Can I Keep a Credit Card Out of Bankruptcy?

Will I be Able to Get a Credit Card After Bankruptcy?

Believe it or not yes. Creditor companies often send debtors offers for credit cards after they filed for bankruptcy knowing that it will be 8 years before they can file for bankruptcy again. Additionally, bankruptcy will illuminate all of your unsecured debt making your debt

Credit Repair is very specialized in many situations. If you need personal guidance on a specific issue you can call me. My phone number and information is on **PAGE 156.**
 My Experience: Finance Degree, 6 years loans officer at a national bank, 4 1/2 years credit bureau manager for one of the big three credit bureau's   John D. Harris

to income ratio more attractive to lenders who see that you now have the ability to take on new debt. This is not to say that filing for bankruptcy is good for your credit, because it is not. However, consumers emerging from bankruptcy commonly receive offers for cards in the mail very soon after their bankruptcy case has closed.

The Bottom Line

the bottom line is that as long as you're acting good faith credit card debt will be discharged in a bankruptcy filing. In fact, one of the main reasons why consumers are forced into bankruptcy is high-interest credit card debt. If you're facing credit card bills that have spiraled out-of-control, it is never a bad idea to meet with a bankruptcy attorney to discuss your options.

As I said before BANKRUPTCY is a great way out.

Decrease your Credit Utilization

Credit use ratio accounts for 30 percent of your score

This is **SO IMPORTANT.** Here is how it works.

Now let's look a 2 different people

John Doe

Peter Smith

They have exactly the same items on their credit reports except

John has a credit card with a limit of $10,000 on it and owes $7000. He has a great job making $125,000 a year and pays on time every month.

Peter has the exact same items on his credit but he has a credit card from the same company but his limit is $1000 because he is unemployed. He owes $100 on it and pays on time every month.

Who has a much better score?

Its Peter because of the Credit Utilization. He is only using 10% of his available credit.

While John is using 70%.

This is so important with your Fico Score. It means so much I have to stress this point. It makes up 30% or more of your score.

But in reality it can jump you from a 580 to a 680.

Credit Utilization Components

The credit utilization category has six subcomponents:

The amount of debt still owed to lenders.

The number of accounts with debt outstanding.

The amount of debt owed on individual accounts.

The lack of a certain type of loan, in some cases.

The percentage of credit lines in use on revolving accounts, like credit cards.

The percentage of debt still owed on installment loans, like mortgages.

It's the comparison of amount of debt to the credit limit that is crucial.

That ratio goes by several names -- credit utilization ratio, credit-limit-to-debt ratio, balance-to-limit ratio and debt-to-available-credit ratio among them

-- but the math is simple. It's the percentage of how much you owe compared to the

amount of your credit limit. If you owe $100 on your credit card and have a $1,000 credit limit on it, your ratio is 10 percent.

Simple, right? Not always. Here's where it gets tricky:

First of all, FICO doesn't view all account types as being equal. "Revolving balances (e.g., credit and retail cards) tend to carry more weight than installment debt (e.g., mortgage, auto and student loans) when amounts owed are considered,"

That means that within the amounts owed category, credit cards are the most important type of account for achieving a high FICO score, but they can also do more damage than other types of credit.

Additionally, while you might consider closing an unused or unwanted credit card to be a smart financial decision, because of the way your utilization ratio is calculated, the FICO score doesn't see it that way.

As an example, imagine you have two credit cards, each with a $500 credit limit, for total available credit of $1,000.

One of the cards hasn't been used for a while and has a zero balance, while the other card has a balance of $250. That gives you a utilization ratio of 25 percent -- your $250 balance divided by your total $1,000 credit limit. You then close that unused card, eliminating the $500 credit limit associated with that account. Now, you've only got $500 in total credit available on that one card, but you still have $250 in debt.

Suddenly, your credit utilization ratio has jumped to 50 percent.

That change can drag down your FICO score -- despite your good intentions. People think closing your cards was always a good thing.

However, when it comes to credit scoring, "Common sense doesn't always work.

It's not only your own actions that can change that utilization ratio for the worse. The bank may also take steps that have a negative impact on a cardholder's FICO score.

Some people have seen a score go down because an issuer had cut a credit line or closed their card for nonuse.

As in the example above, those changes can make it look like the borrower is closer to maxing out their line of credit, which can weigh on a borrower's FICO score.

Ace your credit utilization

To improve the amounts owed portion of your FICO score, start by finding out how much credit you have available. Then, pay down balances. If you're a good customer, the banks may also grant requests to increase your revolving credit lines. An old rule of thumb used to say keep your credit utilization below 30 percent, but that's a myth. There's no magic about 30 percent. Your score won't plummet at 31 percent or soar at 29 percent. The real rule? The lower the utilization, the better.

That can be especially tough for borrowers who only have one account. "If you've got one credit card with a $1,000 line, it's not that hard to hit 30 percent," since you'd only need to carry a balance of $300.

But if you max out a credit card account by using up an entire line of credit, expect your FICO score to drop by 10 to 45 points.

Another danger comes from joint account holders or authorized users who put excessive charges on your shared card. If the other cardholder maxes out a shared account, your FICO score may fall.

Another recommendation? Consider making payments to creditors more than once each month. Otherwise, if you put a major expense -- like a new appliance -- on a credit card, even if you plan to pay it off, your FICO score may take a hit. The reason is that credit scores are calculated as a snapshot in time, so if that happens to be right after you charged a new $700 washing machine, your utilization ratio will look worryingly high.

Things to do to for Best Credit Utilization

It's all about the credit cards.

If you have a credit card you don't use, start using it a little. Around 10% of the limit.

Call all your credit card companies and ask for a large increase to your limit.

Credit Repair is very specialized in many situations. If you need personal guidance on a specific issue you can call me. My phone number and information is on **PAGE 156.**

My Experience: Finance Degree, 6 years loans officer at a national bank, 4 1/2 years credit bureau manager for one of the big three credit bureau's   John D. Harris

Pay your credit cards down to 10% with a loan against your house. If you have equity in your home get a Home Equity Line of Credit.

A home equity line of credit (often called HELOC and pronounced Hee-lock) is a loan in which the lender agrees to lend a maximum amount within an agreed period (called a term), where the collateral is the borrower's equity in his/her house (akin to a second mortgage).

The rates for these are extremely low.

Your credit will sky rocket.

Go to : lendingtree.com and shop for the best rate.

Now let's say you are buying a house and have $25,000 down and have credit cards that are maxed out with $5000 limit.

You are ten times better to pay your cards down to $500.

Put down $20,500 on house instead. Your Fico will sky rocket and you will get a much better interest rate.

Whatever you do get your card balances low.   Everyone can smell a dying fish.

Add credit lines that report to the credit bureaus.

This goes hand and hand with credit utilization because it decrease your debt load.

First check your creditkarma.com for "recommendations". These will always be cards that you are approved for based on your credit score.

Apply for all the cards they show. You will be approved.

Go to creditcards.com and apply for cards for bad credit.

Here are some:

Capital One® Secured MasterCard®

No annual fee, and all the credit building benefits with responsible card use

Unlike a prepaid card, it builds credit when used responsibly, with regular reporting to the 3 major credit bureaus

Credit One® Unsecured Visa® Card

Credit Repair is very specialized in many situations. If you need personal guidance on a specific issue you can call me. My phone number and information is on **PAGE 156.**

My Experience: Finance Degree, 6 years loans officer at a national bank, 4 1/2 years credit bureau manager for one of the big three credit bureau's   John D. Harris

Interested in growing or rebuilding your credit? We report monthly to all three major credit bureaus. Take advantage of free online access to your credit score and credit report summary.

See if you're Pre-Qualified in less than 60 second's

First PREMIER® Bank MasterCard® Credit Card

Checking account required

Apply today and if approved, pay a Processing Fee and you could begin enjoying a manageable credit limit (subject to available credit, additional fees and charges).
Fair/Bad Credit

First PREMIER® Bank Credit Card

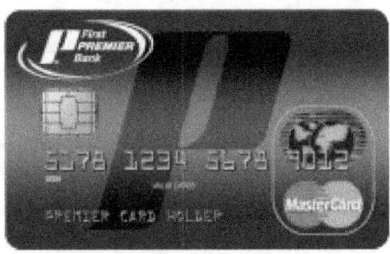

Must have checking account to qualify.

Apply today, and if approved, pay a Processing Fee and you could begin enjoying a manageable credit limit (subject to available credit, additional fees and charges)

Credit One Bank® Cash Back Rewards

Get Pre-Qualified without harming your credit score.

This is a fully functional, unsecured credit card - not a debit, prepaid, or secured card. No need to load funds or tie up cash in deposits. There are no out-of-pocket costs to open your account.

First PREMIER® Bank Classic Credit Card

Must have checking account to qualify

Apply today, and if approved, pay a Processing Fee to access your available credit (additional fees and charges apply).

Credit Repair is very specialized in many situations. If you need personal guidance on a specific issue you can call me. My phone number and information is on **PAGE 156.**

My Experience: Finance Degree, 6 years loans officer at a national bank, 4 1/2 years credit bureau manager for one of the big three credit bureau's   John D. Harris

First PREMIER® Bank Gold Credit Card

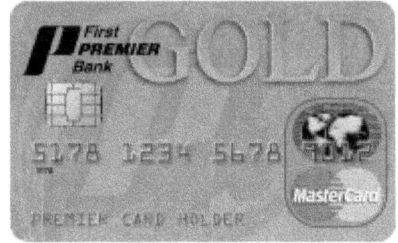

Must have checking account to qualify

Apply today and if approved, pay a Processing Fee and you could begin enjoying a manageable credit limit (subject to available credit, additional fees and charges).

Surge MasterCard® Credit Card

Initial Credit Limit of $500.00* (subject to available credit)

Monthly reporting to the three major credit bureaus

Credit One® Unsecured Platinum Visa® Card

Get Pre-Qualified without affecting your credit score

This is a fully unsecured credit card with no deposit requirement

Group One Freedom Card

$500 Unsecured line of Credit

Reports to major credit bureau

Capital One® Platinum Credit Card

Pay no annual fee

Get access to a higher credit line after making your first 5 monthly payments on time

Capital One® QuicksilverOne® Cash Rewards

Credit Repair is very specialized in many situations. If you need personal guidance on a specific issue you can call me. My phone number and information is on **PAGE 156.**
My Experience: Finance Degree, 6 years loans officer at a national bank, 4 1/2 years credit bureau manager for one of the big three credit bureau's   John D. Harris

Earn unlimited 1.5% cash back on every purchase, every day

No rotating categories or sign ups needed to earn cash rewards; plus, cash back doesn't expire and there's no limit to how much you can earn

Barclaycard Rewards MasterCard®

2X points on purchases for gas, groceries and utilities, and 1X points on all other purchases

No annual fee

Chase Slate®

Chase Slate named "Best Credit Card for Balance Transfers" three years in a row by MONEY Magazine

$0 Introductory balance transfer fee for transfers made during the first 60 days

Credit One Bank® Platinum Visa® Rewards Card

Credit One Bank® Platinum Visa®

Automatic reviews for credit line increase opportunities

Get Pre-Qualified without harming your credit score

First PREMIER® Bank MasterCard® Credit Card

Checking account required

Apply today and if approved, pay a Processing Fee and you could begin enjoying a manageable credit limit (subject to available credit, additional fees and charges).

Credit Repair is very specialized in many situations. If you need personal guidance on a specific issue you can call me. My phone number and information is on **PAGE 156.**
My Experience: Finance Degree, 6 years loans officer at a national bank, 4 1/2 years credit bureau manager for one of the big three credit bureau's   John D. Harris

Indigo® Platinum MasterCard®

Choose your card design - Free

Pre-qualification available with no impact to your credit score

Credit One® Rewards Card

Credit One automatically monitors every account for credit line increase opportunities. We'll let you know as soon as you're eligible for additional credit.

See if you're Pre-Qualified without harming your credit score. In less than 60 seconds, find the card that's right for you.

Add Secured Credit Lines that Report to the Credit Bureaus.

What is a Secured Line

The biggest difference between a secured and an unsecured credit card is that secured cards typically require a security deposit from the cardholder, which functions as cash collateral against you defaulting on your payments.

Secured credit cards are especially useful for consumers with poor or little to no credit history who are typically declined for unsecured credit cards. A secured card can almost guarantee approval by the lending institution because, in effect, you are the one taking on the financial risk through your security deposit.

Think of a secured card as your credit line "training wheels" that allow you the benefits of owning a credit card while giving you the opportunity to build a history of responsible credit use with on-time payments. The small credit limits and security deposit requirements are there to protect you from getting yourself into the poor payment history that may have plagued you in the past.

Secured card credit limits are often set at the amount of the security deposit or some percentage of it so that you cannot charge more than your security deposit can cover. Depending on your specific secured card, adding more to your security deposit enables you to access a higher credit limit, or if your payments are on-time and consistent, the credit card company may reward you by increasing your credit line without requiring additional deposits.

Many secured cards increase the credit limit of your secured card after 6-12 months of responsible use and on-time payments.

Here are some:

Capital One® Secured MasterCard®

No annual fee, and all the credit building benefits with responsible card use

Unlike a prepaid card, it builds credit when used responsibly, with regular reporting to the 3 major credit bureaus

Discover it® Secured Credit Card

No annual fee. No late fee on your first late payment. No increase to your APR for paying late.*

Credit Repair is very specialized in many situations. If you need personal guidance on a specific issue you can call me. My phone number and information is on **PAGE 156.**
My Experience: Finance Degree, 6 years loans officer at a national bank, 4 1/2 years credit bureau manager for one of the big three credit bureau's   John D. Harris

Earn 2% cash back at restaurants & gas stations on up to $1,000 in combined purchases each quarter. Earn 1% cash back on all other purchases.

OpenSky® Secured Visa® Credit Card

Build Your Credit fast with our monthly reporting to all 3 major credit bureaus.

Choose your credit line as low as $200 up to $3000, secured by a fully-refundable* security deposit.

First Progress Platinum Prestige MasterCard® Secured Credit Card

Fund your new MasterCard® secured credit card with your tax refund today!

Our card reports monthly to all three major bureaus and approval is based upon a fully-refundable security deposit.

Citi® Secured MasterCard®

Start building credit for tomorrow

A security deposit is required for this product (minimum $200)

Primor® Secured Visa Classic Card

Credit lines available from $200 to $5,000! You decide where you want to start and open your Personal Savings Deposit Account to secured your line

Guaranteed Approval* as long as your monthly income exceeds your monthly expenses by $100 or more!*

Primor® Secured Visa Gold Card

Low fixed 9.99% interest rate on purchases! Guaranteed Approval* as long as your monthly income exceeds your monthly expenses by $100 or more!*

Credit Repair is very specialized in many situations. If you need personal guidance on a specific issue you can call me. My phone number and information is on **PAGE 156.**
My Experience: Finance Degree, 6 years loans officer at a national bank, 4 1/2 years credit bureau manager for one of the big three credit bureau's   John D. Harris

Credit lines available from $200 to $5,000! You decide where you want to start and open your Personal Savings Deposit Account to secured your line

First Progress Platinum Elite MasterCard® Secured Credit Card

Fund your new MasterCard® secured credit card with your tax refund today!

Receive Your Card More Quickly with New Expedited Processing Option

UNITY® Visa Secured Credit Card - The Comeback Card™

Limited Time Offer: New card members get a $25 rebate* - To be eligible, applications must be submitted

Apply online in less than 5 minutes, and you could be approved today!

First PREMIER® Bank Secured Credit Card

If approved, fund your Security Deposit to open your account. Once open, you will have the opportunity to build your credit limit up to $5,000.

This is a genuine secured credit card - not a debit or prepaid card.

Get a Piggy Back Account

A "piggybacker," more commonly known as an "authorized user," is a person permitted to use a credit card by a primary cardholder who maintains responsibility for all debt on the card, regardless of who makes the charges. Authorized users are typically -- though not always, as you'll see -- a spouse, partner, child, relative or friend of the primary account holder.

The term "piggybacking" refers to the way in which the entire credit history of an account is not only included in the primary cardholder's credit report and score, but also becomes part of the authorized user's report and score. this happens whether the card is actually used by the authorized user or not.

In recent years, piggybacking has become one of the more popular, and at the same time controversial, ways of building credit for someone who is either new to credit or recovering from financial setbacks. Popular, due to the ease with which an authorized user can be added to an account -- no credit requirements -- and the immediate scoring benefit that can be realized from the primary cardholder's (hopefully) positive credit history. Controversial, in that someone who has not used, not managed, or has even misused credit in the past, can reap the scoring benefit of a seasoned and well-managed card without having truly done anything to earn the additional scoring points that can accompany the account. For example, a young person piggybacking on a parent's long-held and well maintained card can, without having any credit of her own, achieve a very good credit score based on a credit history older than she!

But, the piggybacking picture is not all win-win for authorized users.

Since the card history -- good or bad -- is included in the authorized user's credit report and credit score, it behooves the authorized user to make sure the card is always paid on time and maintains low credit utilization (card balance/limit percentage). Otherwise, piggybacking could backfire and result in a worse credit score than you'd have without being an authorized user on the card. In fact, consider this to be just one more of the many good reasons to check your credit reports.

Fortunately, should you discover that the primary account holder is not managing the account to your liking, you can have yourself removed from the account -- preferably by having the primary account holder contact the lender -- and have it removed from your credit report by disputing it as "not mine" with the credit bureaus.

Perhaps the most controversial aspect of piggybacking in recent years has been the use of this feature to artificially inflate credit scores for profit via a purely business-only relationship in which the piggybacker, often a complete stranger, pays to be added as an authorized user without receiving a card or participating in the managing the account in any way.

In an attempt to head off such piggybacking abuse, the FICO 8 credit score, launched in 2009, initially excluded accounts held as an authorized user from scoring. FICO quickly reversed course, however, and went back to allowing piggybacking in scores -- but with an adjustment to generate fewer points for accounts held as an authorized user than as a primary account holder. It had become apparent to FICO that the price for discouraging piggybacking abuse by a relative few would be the denial of honestly-earned credit history for millions of legitimate authorized users -- most often the spouses of primary cardholders -- who use and manage these accounts no differently than those in the primary role.

You should consider the authorized user option as an easy-to-implement, minimal-risk way to build or rebuild credit

Add Your Utilities and Rent

Now you can't actually add your utility bills and rent to your Fico but you can add it to your PRBC score which you can show lenders.

Before you take out a loan or make a big purchase, lenders will want to be sure you'll make your payments. Having a good credit score tells them you're reliable. The trouble is, traditional scores don't include some of your most important payment habits. That means you could be paying all of your bills on time, every month, but still be denied a loan. With PRBC, those "other" bill payments are part of the decision.

To get a PRBC Score and Report, become a member and register at least three monthly-billed accounts. These might be your rent, your electric bill, your cable bill or even an online service. Then, all you have to do is be sure to pay your bills on time every month. When you do, your good habits show up as a good PRBC Score.

The more accounts you add, and keep up your payments on, the higher your PRBC Score will go. And best of all, getting started on the road to better credit is absolutely free.

You can do this at:
www.prbc.com

Add All Your Good Standing Accounts

Now check all your reports and make sure all off your reports are showing all your good accounts.

Your good accounts might only be showing on one or two bureau's.

If you find any of these accounts here is how to add the good account.

Enclose any documentation that verifies information you're providing.

Credit Repair is very specialized in many situations. If you need personal guidance on a specific issue you can call me. My phone number and information is on **PAGE 156.**
My Experience: Finance Degree, 6 years loans officer at a national bank, 4 1/2 years credit bureau manager for one of the big three credit bureau's   John D. Harris

Sample Add Account Letter

To Whom It May Concern

,According to the Fair Credit Reporting Act, 15 USC section 1681i, I request that you add the following credit accounts to my credit report:

Company Name
: [Name of Company]

Account Number
: [Account Number]

Account Type
: [Account Type]

Phone Number
: [Phone Number]

Date
: [Date]

I appreciate your attention to this matter, Please inform me within the statutory 30-day time period from your receipt of The purpose of this credit repair letter of your compliance with the provisions described in 15 USC 1681e,which require that all information in a consumer's credit report must reflect the maximum possible level of accuracy".

[Name]
Social Security Number: [Social Security Number]
Date of Birth: [Date of Birth]
[Current Address]:[City, State Zip]Sincerely,

[Signature]
[Date
IN WITNESS WHEREOF, the said party has signed and sealed these presents the day and year first above written. Signed, sealed and delivered in the presence of:
{PRINT YOUR NAME HERE} _____ Signature
STATE OF
COUNTY OF
I HEREBY CERTIFY that on this day before me, an officer duly qualified to take acknowledgments, personally appeared
{   YOUR   NAME   HERE   },   who   has   produced
_____ as identification and who executed the foregoing instrument and he/she acknowledged before me that he/she executed the same.
WITNESS my hand and official seal in the County and State aforesaid this _____ day of _____2016.

_____ Notary Public
Printed Name

104

My commission expires:

---------------------End of Letter.
Add Your Identification Form

Identification Form

Copy Driver's License

Bill addressed to you

Pay check stub with your address on it

On the bottom of this   "ID DOCUMENT"

I declare under penalty of perjury (under the laws of the United States of America) that this identification provide is me
John Doe
Signature
Date

Credit Repair is very specialized in many situations. If you need personal guidance on a specific issue you can call me. My phone number and information is on **PAGE 156.**
My Experience: Finance Degree, 6 years loans officer at a national bank, 4 1/2 years credit bureau manager for one of the big three credit bureau's   John D. Harris

Now Get it Notarized

Now you need to get the letter(s) notarized.   You will add a copy of your social security card and Driver License (or passport) for proof of your identity and go a notary of the public. DO NOT SIGN THE LETTERS UNTIL YOU GO TO THE NOTARY AND THEY TELL YOU TO SIGN IT.

Now Track Your letters

Now your letters are ready to send. You will send your letter WITH TRACKING Certified Mail. This is your proof that CRA's get your letter(s).

This is an absolute must.

File all your paperwork

Here are the addresses you need to send the letters.

Equifax
P.O. Box 740256 Atlanta, GA 30374-0256
Experian
P.O. Box 2106 Allen, TX 75013
TransUnion
P.O. Box 34012 Fullerton, CA 92634

Make sure your address and employer are the same that the credit bureau has for you.

If this information is not correct change it on your credit report.

Login to your credit karma and Experian account and update your personal information. Make sure its updated before you send your letters. They are usually very quick with personal information updates.

Deleting Items From Your Report

Reports Have Errors

Credit Repair is very specialized in many situations. If you need personal guidance on a specific issue you can call me. My phone number and information is on **PAGE 156.**
My Experience: Finance Degree, 6 years loans officer at a national bank, 4 1/2 years credit bureau manager for one of the big three credit bureau's   John D. Harris

79 percent of all credit reports contain some type of error - and 25 percent contain such serious errors that those individuals could be denied credit.

Here are other significant findings:

54 percent contained inaccurate personal information such as misspelled names, wrong Social Security numbers, inaccurate birth dates, inaccurate information about a spouse and out of date address. For example, one credit report listed a man's business partner as his spouse.
30 percent listed "closed" accounts as "open." For example, listing a student loan that was paid off years ago as still outstanding. Another report listed several credit cards, a mortgage and an auto loan all as open.
22 percent of reports had the same mortgage or loan listed twice. This mistake often occurs when loans are serviced or sold.
8 percent of reports simply didn't list major credit, loan, mortgage or other accounts that could be used to demonstrate the creditworthiness of a consumer.

These errors can create the appearance of a consumer having "too much" credit available, being over-extended, or not having been a responsible payer of his or her obligations.

The "big three" credit report bureaus - Equifax, Experian and TransUnion - have been in this business for years, so how can they possibly be making all of these mistakes?

Most mistakes can be pinned to your creditors and others providing info to the credit bureaus. As mentioned above, some mistakes happen when credit accounts change hands. Some errors are intentional. The report found that some banks admit to not furnishing bureaus with complete information on customers.

Other mistakes are simply human error. According to a credit bureau industry spokesman, some 30,000 data processors file 4.5 billion updates to credit reports each month, leaving considerable room for errors.

These errors on credit reports can cause consumers serious trouble. Many consumers probably don't realize just how serious.

Are the Debts Yours?

Now make sure they are actually not your debts. This is important just so you know who you are dealing with.

For example all creditors sell their debts to third parties. So Here is a debt showing up on a TransUnion credit report:

Collection Account Example 1

Account Details

Last Reported

Apr 26, 2015

Collection Agency

ERC

Original Creditor

11 AT T

Status

Open

Opened Date

Mar 09, 2015

Closed Date

--

Responsibility

Individual

Balance

$59

High Balance

$59

Remarks

Placed for collection

Creditor Contact Details

ENHANCED RECOVERY COMPAN

PO BOX 57547

JACKSONVILLE, FL

Credit Repair is very specialized in many situations. If you need personal guidance on a specific issue you can call me. My phone number and information is on **PAGE 156.**
My Experience: Finance Degree, 6 years loans officer at a national bank, 4 1/2 years credit bureau manager for one of the big three credit bureau's   John D. Harris

32241

(800) 496-8941

NOW YOU DON'T KNOW THE COMPANY "ENHANCED RECOVERY COMPANY BUT IF YOU SEE THE ORIGINAL DEBTOR IS AT&T YOU MIGHT KNOW THEM.

Collection Account Example 2

CMRE FINANCIAL SERVICES

MED1 02 MEDICAL PAYMENT DATA

Jul 17, 2014

Open

$472

Account Details

Last Reported

Nov 21, 2015

Collection Agency

CMRE FINANCIAL SERVICES

Original Creditor

MED1 02 MEDICAL PAYMENT DATA

Status

Open

Opened Date

Jul 17, 2014

Closed Date

--

Responsibility

Individual

Balance

$472

High Balance

$416

Remarks

Placed for collection

Creditor Contact Details

CMRE FINANCIAL SERVICES

3075 E IMPERIAL HW 200

BREA, CA

92821

(877) 572-7555

Credit Repair is very specialized in many situations. If you need personal guidance on a specific issue you can call me. My phone number and information is on **PAGE 156.**
My Experience: Finance Degree, 6 years loans officer at a national bank, 4 1/2 years credit bureau manager for one of the big three credit bureau's   John D. Harris

Now the original creditor here is CMRE FINANCIAL SERVICES. They are not a company that is easily recognized but you might have had a service done. In this case it was an X-Ray.

Setting up Your Folders Like This:

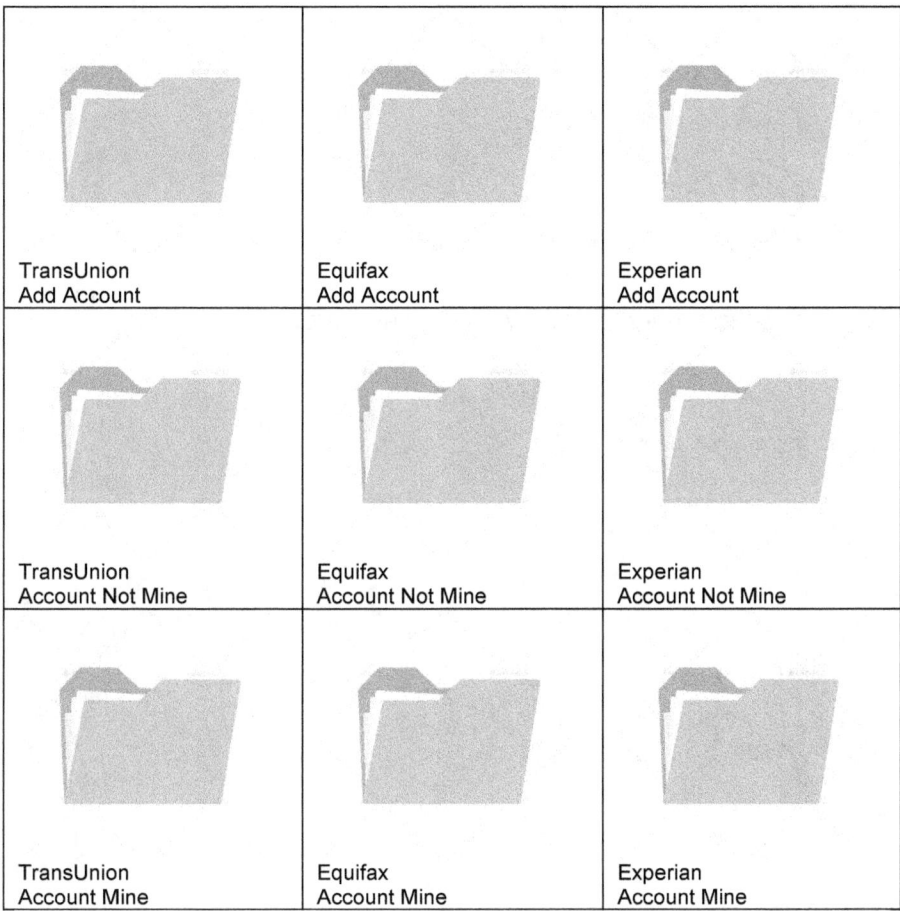

TransUnion Add Account	Equifax Add Account	Experian Add Account
TransUnion Account Not Mine	Equifax Account Not Mine	Experian Account Not Mine
TransUnion Account Mine	Equifax Account Mine	Experian Account Mine

Add Account folder is for accounts you want to add.

Accounts Not Mine are accounts you don't believe are yours. Look into these accounts before you file them in this folder.

Accounts Mine are accounts you recognize but want to delete anyway.

Credit Repair is very specialized in many situations. If you need personal guidance on a specific issue you can call me. My phone number and information is on **PAGE 156.**
My Experience: Finance Degree, 6 years loans officer at a national bank, 4 1/2 years credit bureau manager for one of the big three credit bureau's   John D. Harris

Print a Copy of all Accounts on Your Credit Reports

That You are Going to Add or Dispute

Print a copy of the debt and file it in the appropriate folder.

BEFORE YOU FILE THE DEBT CALL AND GET THE ACCOUNT NUMBER.

So with this example debt

Account Details
Last Reported

Apr 26, 2015

Collection Agency

ERC

Original Creditor

411 AT T

Status

Open

Opened Date

Mar 09, 2015

Closed Date

--

Responsibility

Individual

Balance

$59

High Balance

$59

Remarks

Placed for collection

Creditor Contact Details

ENHANCED RECOVERY COMPAN

PO BOX 57547

JACKSONVILLE, FL

32241

(800) 496-8941

First you should call ATT

If that doesn't work you would call:

Creditor Contact Details
ENHANCED RECOVERY COMPAN
PO BOX 57547
JACKSONVILLE, FL
32241
(800) 496-8941

Sample Call to Original Creditor

Your phone call should go like this: Hello I saw this debt on my credit report that I'm not sure is mine. If it is mine I am willing to pay it. What is the account number from the AT&T account so I can check my records. My social # is 645-98-9876.

After you get the account number for the original debt write it on your debt page.

Credit Repair is very specialized in many situations. If you need personal guidance on a specific issue you can call me. My phone number and information is on **PAGE 156.**

My Experience: Finance Degree, 6 years loans officer at a national bank, 4 1/2 years credit bureau manager for one of the big three credit bureau's   John D. Harris

Sample Call to Collection Company

THE COLLECTION COMPANY. BLOCK YOUR PHONE NUMBER. You don't want them calling you. Do not give them information but get the account# for the original debt if you don't know it.

Your phone call should go like this: Hello I saw this debt on my credit report that I'm not sure is mine. If it is mine I am willing to pay it. What is the account number from the AT&T account so I can check my records.

Many times they will say your account number is not with AT&T anymore It's with them, don't take that answer. You need the account number for the original creditor because you don't want to pay someone else's debt.

After you get the account number for the original debt write it on your debt page.

Make sure you check with AT&T that the number they gave you is an account number with them.

The Secret to Disputing Accounts

What you should have done

9 Folders
Experian-Add Account
Experian-Account Not Mine
Experian-Account Mine

Equifax-Add Account
Equifax-Account Not Mine
Equifax-Account Mine

TransUnion-Add Account
TransUnion-Not Mine
TransUnion-Account Mine

You should now have a printed a copy of all your debts with the original account number. You should also have accounts you want to add.

If you haven't don't have these things done go back and do them. This is absolutely necessary.

Review-Set up Your Folders Like This:

Credit Repair is very specialized in many situations. If you need personal guidance on a specific issue you can call me. My phone number and information is on **PAGE 156.**
My Experience: Finance Degree, 6 years loans officer at a national bank, 4 1/2 years credit bureau manager for one of the big three credit bureau's   John D. Harris

TransUnion Add Account	Equifax Add Account	Experian Add Account
TransUnion Account Not Mine	Equifax Account Not Mine	Experian Account Not Mine
TransUnion Account Mine	Equifax Account Mine	Experian Account Mine

Never Dispute Things Online

I NEED TO SAY THIS AGAIN AND AGAIN NEVER DISPUTE ANYTHING ONLINE.

3 Reasons You Should Never Dispute Credit Errors Online

Reason Number One: Time

One important factor you have on your side when disputing errors in your credit report is time. By law, the credit bureaus have 30 days within receipt of that dispute to properly investigate your claim. However, this only applies to reports other than one obtained for free at annualcreditreport.com. In that case, the credit bureaus have 45 days to respond.

Like I told you before don't get your report from annualcreditreport.com

Reason Number Two: Shortcut The Process

The Credit Bureaus online dispute system is set up in such a way that when you use it, it makes their job that much easier. The information you put into their limited dispute fields falls right into their electronic verification system. By using their online dispute system (E-OSCAR), **you have no proof of the dispute or a paper trail that certified return receipt requested would give you if you had mailed that dispute.** An important aspect of accelerating the credit recovery process is keeping meticulous records.

If you catch the credit bureaus in violation of the Fair Credit Reporting Act or a collection company in violation of the Fair Debt Collection Practices Act, you'll have the necessary ammunition to beat them in court and clear your good name should you have to go that route.

Reason Number Three: Revision Not In Your Favor

When the Fair Credit Reporting Act was revised by FACTA, they put in a section for "Expedited Dispute Resolution" Section 611a(8), also known as the on-line dispute system. If you read this section, you will notice the following;

Well paragraph 2 is the part that requires the CRA to forward your dispute and all related documentation you provide to the creditor or company furnishing the information to the bureau. Paragraph 6 is the part that requires the CRA to provide you with written results of the re-investigation. And paragraph 7 is the part that requires the CRA to provide you with the method of verification on request by you, the consumer.

So as you can see, by using the CRA'S online disputing system (E-OSCAR), which by the way stands for Electronic Online System for Complete and Accurate Reporting (lol), you wouldn't receive a notice from the credit bureaus telling you that the information you disputed has been verified as accurate, which, by receiving this notice is what allows you to request the method of verification (MOV). The credit bureau then must provide you with this information within 15 days of your request.

Important Tool

As you can see, Method of Verification is another important tool to use and a very important part of accelerating the process of credit recovery should you need to delete an item discovered to be in error, incomplete, or unverifiable during the "Credit Audit and Verification" process. So why would you give these rights up; voluntarily no less?

Credit Repair is very specialized in many situations. If you need personal guidance on a specific issue you can call me. My phone number and information is on **PAGE 156.**
My Experience: Finance Degree, 6 years loans officer at a national bank, 4 1/2 years credit bureau manager for one of the big three credit bureau's   John D. Harris

Additionally, the law is not specific enough and does not say "permanently delete or suppress"; herein lays the problem. The Credit Reporting Agencies (CRA) can "soft delete" a disputed trade line for 30 days and then the trade line can reappear when the furnisher (creditor or collector) reports it again in the next 30 day cycle. This is due to the fact that the CRA's are not required to tell the creditor or collector that you disputed it at all, thanks to the "shall not be required to comply with paragraphs 2" if you decide to dispute an item online. Are you getting all of this?

This is a deceptive system in where you, the Amateur Consumer, think you may have succeeded in your dispute and gotten what is known as a "hard delete", but in fact, it is only temporary. Since the creditor or furnisher of that information does not know the item was deleted, they will mistakenly re-report it and then conveniently, the credit bureau will place the negative item back on your report. And if that isn't bad enough, you lose the hard copy of the investigation results you would otherwise have received and been entitled to if the dispute had been sent via certified mail in the first place.

Again, by disputing in writing, as the FTC states you should on their website, the bureaus might temporarily remove a negative item (soft delete) until the information is verified as true but...if the information is verified to be true, they must then notify you in writing within 5 days of putting the item back on your credit report. If they don't, it's a violation of the FCRA and you could potentially sue them for $1,000.

Listen To The FTC

Look, there's a reason why the FTC states right there on its website that you should dispute EVERY item you think is not accurate, incomplete, or unverifiable on your credit in writing and by certified mail, "return receipt requested"; it's because you are protected as a consumer and by disputing online electronically, you lose many rights under FCRA. So why would you ever do this

Two Means of Disputes

1) Disputing with the credit bureau.
2) Disputing with the collection company/original debtor

You have rights in both these situations. Let's get ready to remove those negative items.

Disputing with the Credit Bureaus

Many of the adverse items on a credit report may in fact be true.

So, if you were to dispute the adverse items with a traditional dispute process most of those accounts will be "verified" and will stay on your credit report thus in turn keeping your FICO score down.

That is NOT what you are going to do.

SECTION 609 of the Fair Credit Reporting Act does not care whether the negative account is valid or not. The letter disputes the CRA's right to REPORT the adverse account –

NOT whether or not the adverse account is valid. These letters will request, under SECTION 609 of the Fair Credit Reporting Act, that the CRA's send you a copy of the original contract that you signed – that they are supposed to have.

If they are verifying the account as being valid/correct then they, by law, are supposed to have a copy of that contract to do so. THEY DON'T. And since they don't they can't provide you a copy nor can they legally verify the account.

Under the Fair Credit Reporting Act they must provide you a copy if you request it. Since they will not be able to provide you such a document the account will be UNVERIFIED and under Federal Law any UNVERIFIED accounts must be deleted.

Disputing with the Bureaus Must Do's

1)First you should hand write all your letters ok I know this seems like a lot of work but it's worth it. You have to be the customer who is really disputing an item. You are not using a website template. You have hand written your letters.

2)All Letters have to be notarized.

Credit Repair is very specialized in many situations. If you need personal guidance on a specific issue you can call me. My phone number and information is on **PAGE 156.**
 My Experience: Finance Degree, 6 years loans officer at a national bank, 4 1/2 years credit bureau manager for one of the big three credit bureau's   John D. Harris

3)All letters have to be sent registered mail.

4)All letters have to include your "Identification Form"

5) Dispute 2 items with each bureau at a time.

Dispute Addresses

Experian's mailing address for dispute requests is:
P.O. Box 4500
Allen, TX 75013

Equifax Information Services LLC
P.O. Box 740256
Atlanta, GA 30374

TransUnion Consumer Solutions
P.O. Box 2000
Chester, PA 19022-2000

Always mail to these addresses.

Include this form with letters to Equifax
http://www.equifax.com/cp/MailInDislcosureRequest.pdf

Include this form with letters to TransUnion
https://www.transunion.com/docs/rev/personal/InvestigationRequest.pdf

GENERATION 1.0 LETTER

Your Name
Address
City, State
Zip
SSN: 000-00-0000 | DOB: 1/1/1970

Experian

P.O. Box 4500
Allen, TX 75013

According to the Fair Credit Reporting Section 609 (a)(1)(A), you are required by federal law to verify - through the physical verification of the original signed consumer contract - any and all accounts you post on a credit report.

Otherwise, anyone paying for your reporting services could fax, mail or email in a fraudulent account. I demand to see Verifiable Proof (an original Consumer Contract with my Signature on it) you have on file of the accounts listed below.

Your failure to positively verify these accounts has hurt my ability to obtain credit.

Under the FCRA, unverified accounts must be removed and if you are unable to provide me a copy of verifiable proof, you must remove the accounts listed below.

I demand the following accounts be verified or removed immediately.

Account 1 (AT&T) _____ Account #_____
Account 1 (SPRINT) _____ Account #_____

Please note that I have opted out in writing to your forced arbitration terms and am willing to seek legal relief.

{Print Name}
{Signature}
{Date}

IN WITNESS WHEREOF, the said party has signed and sealed these presents the day and year first above written. Signed, sealed and delivered in the presence of:
 {PRINT YOUR NAME HERE} _____ Signature
 STATE OF
 COUNTY OF
 I HEREBY CERTIFY that on this day before me, an officer duly qualified to take acknowledgments, personally appeared
 {   YOUR   NAME   HERE   },   who   has   produced
_____ as identification and who executed the foregoing instrument and he/she acknowledged before me that he/she executed the same.
 WITNESS my hand and official seal in the County and State aforesaid this _____ day of _____2016.

_____ Notary Public

Printed Name
My commission expires:

----------------------End of Letter.

Identification Form GENERATION 1.0 LETTER

Copy Driver's License

Bill addressed to you

Pay check stub with your address on it

On the bottom of this "ID DOCUMENT"

I declare under penalty of perjury (under the laws of the United States of America) that this
identification provide is me
John Doe
Signature
Date

Credit Repair is very specialized in many situations. If you need personal guidance on a specific issue you can call me. My phone number and information is on **PAGE 156.**
My Experience: Finance Degree, 6 years loans officer at a national bank, 4 1/2 years credit bureau manager for one of the big three credit bureau's   John D. Harris

Now your letter is ready to send. You will send your letter WITH TRACKING Priority Mail. This is your proof that CRA's get your letter(s).

This is an absolute must.

File all your paperwork.

Possible Results

When you send your notarized letters to Equifax, TransUnion, and Experian they might try to ignore you.

They might send you a reply saying a suspicious letter was sent on your behalf but has been ignored or may try to intimidate you to stop you from continuing your disputes.

Here are some responses.

"We received a suspicious request regarding your personal credit information that we have determined was not sent by you. We have not taken any action on this request and any future requests made in this manner will not be processed and will not receive a response."

You might also get something like this: "Suspicious requests are taken seriously and reviewed by security personnel who will report deceptive activity, including copies of letters deemed as suspicious, to law enforcement officials and to state or federal regulatory agencies.

They may also ask for proof of your identity and request you mail them such proof.

You have already sent a notarized letter identification form with "I declare under penalty of perjury (under the laws of the United States of America) that this identification provide is me"

All these responses are great for you. They show that the bureaus are not providing information required and the timeline is ticking.

They are trying to scare you.

Credit Repair is very specialized in many situations. If you need personal guidance on a specific issue you can call me. My phone number and information is on **PAGE 156.**

My Experience: Finance Degree, 6 years loans officer at a national bank, 4 1/2 years credit bureau manager for one of the big three credit bureau's   John D. Harris

They can't do anything to you.

Repeat after me.

They can't scare me.
I will persist and prevail.

They can't scare me.
I will persist and prevail.

They can't scare me.
I will persist and prevail.

GENERATION 2.0 LETTER

Your Name
Address
City, State
Zip
SSN: 000-00-0000 | DOB: 1/1/1970

Experian
P.O. Box 4500
Allen, TX 75013

According to the Fair Credit Reporting Section 609 (a)(1)(A), you are required by federal law to verify - through the physical verification of the original signed consumer contract - any and all accounts you post on a credit report.

Otherwise, anyone paying for your reporting services could fax, mail or email in a fraudulent account. I demand to see Verifiable Proof (an original Consumer Contract with my Signature on it) you have on file of the accounts listed below.

Your failure to positively verify these accounts has hurt my ability to obtain credit.

Under the FCRA, unverified accounts must be removed and if you are unable to provide me a copy of verifiable proof, you must remove the accounts listed below. I demand the following accounts be verified or removed immediately.

Account 1 (AT&T) _____ Account #_____
Account 1 (SPRINT) _____ Account #_____

Please note that I have opted out in writing to your forced arbitration terms and am willing to seek legal relief.

{Print Name}
{Signature}
{Date}

Credit Repair is very specialized in many situations. If you need personal guidance on a specific issue you can call me. My phone number and information is on **PAGE 156.**
My Experience: Finance Degree, 6 years loans officer at a national bank, 4 1/2 years credit bureau manager for one of the big three credit bureau's   John D. Harris

IN WITNESS WHEREOF, the said party has signed and sealed these presents the day and year first above written. Signed, sealed and delivered in the presence of:
{PRINT YOUR NAME HERE} _____ Signature
STATE OF
COUNTY OF
I HEREBY CERTIFY that on this day before me, an officer duly qualified to take acknowledgments, personally appeared
{   YOUR   NAME   HERE   },   who   has   produced
_____ as identification and who executed the foregoing instrument and he/she acknowledged before me that he/she executed the same.
WITNESS my hand and official seal in the County and State aforesaid this _____ day of _____2016.

_____ Notary Public
Printed Name
My commission expires:

--------------------End of Letter.

Identification Form GENERATION 2.0 LETTER

Copy Driver's License

Bill addressed to you

Pay check stub with your address on it

On the bottom of this "ID DOCUMENT"

I declare under penalty of perjury (under the laws of the United States of America) that this identification provide is me
John Doe
Signature
Date

Now your letter is ready to send. You will send your letter WITH TRACKING Priority Mail. This is your proof that CRA's get your letter(s).

This is an absolute must.

Credit Repair is very specialized in many situations. If you need personal guidance on a specific issue you can call me. My phone number and information is on **PAGE 156.**
My Experience: Finance Degree, 6 years loans officer at a national bank, 4 1/2 years credit bureau manager for one of the big three credit bureau's   John D. Harris

File all your paperwork.

GENERATION 3.0 LETTER

Your Name
Address
City, State
Zip
SSN: 000-00-0000 | DOB: 1/1/1970

Experian
P.O. Box 4500
Allen, TX 75013

Please be advised this is my THIRD WRITTEN REQUEST and FINAL WARNING that I fully intend to pursue litigation in accordance with the FCRA to enforce my rights and seek relief and recover all monetary damages that I may be entitled to under Section 616 and Section 617 regarding your continued willful and negligent noncompliance.
Despite two written requests, the unverified items listed below still remain on my credit

report in violation of Federal Law.

You are required under the FCRA to have a copy of the original creditors documentation on file to verify that this information is mine and is correct.

In the results of your first investigation and subsequent reinvestigation, you stated in writing that you "verified" that these items are being "reported correctly" ?

Who verified these accounts? You have NOT provided me a copy of ANY original documentation (a consumer contract with my signature on it) as required under Section 609 (a)(1)(A) & Section 611 (a)(1)(A).

Furthermore you have failed to provide the method of verification as required under Section 611 (a) (7).

Please be advised that under Section 611 (5)(A) of the FCRA – you are required to "...promptly DELETE all information which cannot be verified."

The law is very clear as to the Civil liability and the remedy available to me (Section 616 & 617) if you fail to comply with Federal Law. I am a litigious consumer and fully intend on pursuing litigation in this matter to enforce my rights under the FCRA.

Account 1 (AT&T) _____ Account #_____
Account 1 (SPRINT) _____ Account #_____

Please note that I have opted out in writing to your forced arbitration terms and am willing to seek legal relief.

{Print Name}
{Signature}
{Date}

IN WITNESS WHEREOF, the said party has signed and sealed these presents the day and year first above written. Signed, sealed and delivered in the presence of:
{PRINT YOUR NAME HERE} _____ Signature
STATE OF
COUNTY OF
I HEREBY CERTIFY that on this day before me, an officer duly qualified to take acknowledgments, personally appeared
{ YOUR NAME HERE }, who has produced
_____ as identification and who executed the foregoing instrument and he/she acknowledged before me that he/she executed the same.

WITNESS my hand and official seal in the County and State aforesaid this _____ day of _____2016.

_____ Notary Public

Printed Name
My commission expires:

--------------------End of Letter.

Credit Repair is very specialized in many situations. If you need personal guidance on a specific issue you can call me. My phone number and information is on **PAGE 156.**

My Experience: Finance Degree, 6 years loans officer at a national bank, 4 1/2 years credit bureau manager for one of the big three credit bureau's   John D. Harris

Identification Form GENERATION 3.0 LETTER

Copy Driver's License

Bill addressed to you

Pay check stub with your address on it

On the bottom of this "ID DOCUMENT"

I declare under penalty of perjury (under the laws of the United States of America) that this
identification provide is me
John Doe
Signature
Date

Now your letter is ready to send. You will send your letter WITH TRACKING Priority Mail.
This is your proof that CRA's get your letter(s).

Credit Repair is very specialized in many situations. If you need personal guidance on a specific issue you can call me. My phone number and information is on **PAGE 156.**

My Experience: Finance Degree, 6 years loans officer at a national bank, 4 1/2 years credit bureau manager for one of the big three credit bureau's   John D. Harris

This is an absolute must.

File all your paperwork.

GENERATION 4.0 LETTER

Your Name
Address
City, State
Zip
SSN: 000-00-0000 | DOB: 1/1/1970

Experian
P.O. Box 4500
Allen, TX 75013

NOTICE OF PENDING LITIGATION SEEKING RELIEF AND MONETARY DAMAGES UNDER FCRA SECTION 616 & SECTION 617 Please accept this final written OFFER OF SETTLEMENT BEFORE LITIGATION as my attempt to amicably resolve your continued violation of the Fair Credit Reporting Act regarding your refusal to delete UNVERIFIED information from my consumer file.

I intend to pursue litigation in accordance with the FCRA to seek relief and recover all monetary damages that I may be entitled to under Section 616 and Section 617 if the UNVERIFIED items listed below are not deleted immediately.

A copy of this letter as well as copies of the three written letters sent to you previously will also become part of a formal complaint to the Federal Trade Commission and shall be used as evidence in pending litigation provided you fail to comply with this offer of settlement. Despite three written requests, the unverified items listed below still remain on my credit report in violation of Federal Law.

You are required under the FCRA to have a copy of the original creditors documentation on file to verify that this information is mine and is correct. In the results of your investigations, you stated in writing that you "verified" that these items are being "reported correctly"? Who verified these accounts?

You have NOT provided me a copy of ANY original documentation (a consumer contract with my signature on it) as required under Section 609 (a)(1)(A) & Section 611 (a)(1)(A).

Furthermore you have failed to provide the method of verification as required under Section 611 (a) (7). Please be advised that under Section 611 (5)(A) of the FCRA – you are required to "…promptly DELETE all information which cannot be verified."

The law is very clear as to the Civil liability and the remedy available to me (Section 616 & 617) if you fail to comply with Federal Law. I am a litigious consumer and fully intend on pursuing litigation in this matter to enforce my rights under the FCRA.

Account 1 (AT&T) _____ Account #_____
Account 1 (SPRINT) _____ Account #_____

Please note that I have opted out in writing to your forced arbitration terms and am willing to seek legal relief.

{Print Name}
{Signature}
{Date}

IN WITNESS WHEREOF, the said party has signed and sealed these presents the day and year first above written. Signed, sealed and delivered in the presence of:
{PRINT YOUR NAME HERE} _____ Signature
STATE OF
COUNTY OF
I HEREBY CERTIFY that on this day before me, an officer duly qualified to take acknowledgments, personally appeared
{ YOUR NAME HERE }, who has produced
_____ as identification and who executed the foregoing instrument and he/she acknowledged before me that he/she executed the same.
WITNESS my hand and official seal in the County and State aforesaid this _____ day of _____2016.

_____ Notary Public
Printed Name
My commission expires:

---------------------End of Letter.

Credit Repair is very specialized in many situations. If you need personal guidance on a specific issue you can call me. My phone number and information is on **PAGE 156.**
 My Experience: Finance Degree, 6 years loans officer at a national bank, 4 1/2 years credit bureau manager for one of the big three credit bureau's   John D. Harris

Identification Form GENERATION 4.0 LETTER

On the bottom of this "ID DOCUMENT"

I declare under penalty of perjury (under the laws of the United States of America) that this identification provide is me
John Doe
Signature
Date

Now your letter is ready to send. You will send your letter WITH TRACKING Priority Mail. This is your proof that CRA's get your letter(s).

This is an absolute must.

Credit Repair is very specialized in many situations. If you need personal guidance on a specific issue you can call me. My phone number and information is on **PAGE 156.**
My Experience: Finance Degree, 6 years loans officer at a national bank, 4 1/2 years credit bureau manager for one of the big three credit bureau's   John D. Harris

File all your paperwork.

GENERATION 5.0 LETTER

Your Name
Address

City, State
Zip
SSN: 000-00-0000 | DOB: 1/1/1970

Experian
P.O. Box 4500
Allen, TX 75013

NOTICE OF PENDING LITIGATION SEEKING RELIEF AND MONETARY DAMAGES UNDER FCRA SECTION 616 & SECTION 617 Please accept this final written OFFER OF SETTLEMENT BEFORE LITIGATION as my attempt to amicably resolve your continued violation of the Fair Credit Reporting Act regarding your refusal to delete UNVERIFIED information from my consumer file.

I intend to pursue litigation in accordance with the FCRA to seek relief and recover all monetary damages that I may be entitled to under Section 616 and Section 617 if the UNVERIFIED items listed below are not deleted immediately.

A copy of this letter as well as copies of the three written letters sent to you previously will also become part of a formal complaint to the Federal Trade Commission and shall be used as evidence in pending litigation provided you fail to comply with this offer of settlement. Despite three written requests, the unverified items listed below still remain on my credit report in violation of Federal Law.

You are required under the FCRA to have a copy of the original creditors documentation on file to verify that this information is mine and is correct. In the results of your investigations, you stated in writing that you "verified" that these items are being "reported correctly"? Who verified these accounts?
You have NOT provided me a copy of ANY original documentation (a consumer contract with my signature on it) as required under Section 609 (a)(1)(A) & Section 611 (a)(1)(A).
Furthermore you have failed to provide the method of verification as required under Section 611 (a) (7).   Please be advised that under Section 611 (5)(A) of the FCRA – you are required to "...promptly DELETE all information which cannot be verified."
The law is very clear as to the Civil liability and the remedy available to me (Section 616 & 617) if you fail to comply with Federal Law. I am a litigious consumer and fully intend on pursuing litigation in this matter to enforce my rights under the FCRA.

Account 1 (AT&T) _____ Account #_____
Account 1 (SPRINT) _____   Account #_____

If I don't get proper documentation I will be filling my complaint at:
www.consumerfinance.gov/Complaint/
and
www.ftccomplaintassistant.gov/

Please note that I have opted out in writing to your forced arbitration terms and am willing to seek legal relief.

{Print Name}
{Signature}
{Date}

IN WITNESS WHEREOF, the said party has signed and sealed these presents the day

Credit Repair is very specialized in many situations. If you need personal guidance on a specific issue you can call me. My phone number and information is on **PAGE 156.**
My Experience: Finance Degree, 6 years loans officer at a national bank, 4 1/2 years credit bureau manager for one of the big three credit bureau's   John D. Harris

and year first above written. Signed, sealed and delivered in the presence of:
    {PRINT YOUR NAME HERE} _____ Signature
    STATE OF
    COUNTY OF
    I HEREBY CERTIFY that on this day before me, an officer duly qualified to take acknowledgments, personally appeared
{   YOUR   NAME   HERE   },   who   has   produced
_____   as identification and who
executed the foregoing instrument and he/she acknowledged before me that he/she executed the same.
    WITNESS my hand and official seal in the County and State aforesaid this _____ day of _____2016.

_____ Notary Public
Printed Name
My commission expires:

--------------------End of Letter.

Identification Form GENERATION 5.0 LETTER

142

Copy Driver's License

Bill addressed to you

Pay check stub with your address on it

On the bottom of this "ID DOCUMENT"

I declare under penalty of perjury (under the laws of the United States of America) that this identification provide is me
John Doe
Signature
Date

Now your letter is ready to send. You will send your letter WITH TRACKING Priority Mail. This is your proof that CRA's get your letter(s).

This is an absolute must.

Credit Repair is very specialized in many situations. If you need personal guidance on a specific issue you can call me. My phone number and information is on **PAGE 156.**
My Experience: Finance Degree, 6 years loans officer at a national bank, 4 1/2 years credit bureau manager for one of the big three credit bureau's   John D. Harris

File all your paperwork.

Small Claims Form Included

With this 6ᵗʰ letter enclose a copy of a small claims court filling. Fill it out

completely like you are ready to file it.

Now don't actually file it just fill it out. You can get one for free at your local court house. Name the bureau as the defendant.

What you file against them for:

negligent and willful failure to provide - through the physical verification of the original signed consumer contract - any and all accounts you post on a credit report.
In violation Section 609 (a)(1)(A), FCRA

negligent and willful failure to reinvestigate the disputed entries in violation of sections 611(a), 616, and 617 of the FCRA, 15 U.S.C. §§ 1681i(a), 1681n, 1681o"

GENERATION 6.0 LETTER

Your Name
Address
City, State
Zip
SSN: 000-00-0000 | DOB: 1/1/1970

Experian
P.O. Box 4500

Allen, TX 75013

NOTICE OF PENDING LITIGATION SEEKING RELIEF AND MONETARY DAMAGES UNDER FCRA SECTION 616 & SECTION 617 Please accept this final written OFFER OF SETTLEMENT BEFORE LITIGATION as my attempt to amicably resolve your continued violation of the Fair Credit Reporting Act regarding your refusal to delete UNVERIFIED information from my consumer file.

I intend to pursue litigation in accordance with the FCRA to seek relief and recover all monetary damages that I may be entitled to under Section 616 and Section 617 if the UNVERIFIED items listed below are not deleted immediately.

A copy of this letter as well as copies of the three written letters sent to you previously will also become part of a formal complaint to the Federal Trade Commission and shall be used as evidence in pending litigation provided you fail to comply with this offer of settlement. Despite three written requests, the unverified items listed below still remain on my credit report in violation of Federal Law.

You are required under the FCRA to have a copy of the original creditors documentation on file to verify that this information is mine and is correct. In the results of your investigations, you stated in writing that you "verified" that these items are being "reported correctly"? Who verified these accounts?
You have NOT provided me a copy of ANY original documentation (a consumer contract with my signature on it) as required under Section 609 (a)(1)(A) & Section 611 (a)(1)(A).
Furthermore you have failed to provide the method of verification as required under Section 611 (a) (7).   Please be advised that under Section 611 (5)(A) of the FCRA – you are required to "…promptly DELETE all information which cannot be verified."
The law is very clear as to the Civil liability and the remedy available to me (Section 616 & 617) if you fail to comply with Federal Law. I am a litigious consumer and fully intend on pursuing litigation in this matter to enforce my rights under the FCRA.

Account 1 (AT&T) _____   Account #_____
Account 1 (SPRINT) _____   Account #_____

If I don't get proper documentation I will be filling my complaint at:
www.consumerfinance.gov/Complaint/
and
www.ftccomplaintassistant.gov/

Please note that I have opted out in writing to your forced arbitration terms and am willing to seek legal relief.

{Print Name}
{Signature}
{Date}

IN WITNESS WHEREOF, the said party has signed and sealed these presents the day

146

and year first above written. Signed, sealed and delivered in the presence of:
{PRINT YOUR NAME HERE} _____ Signature
STATE OF
COUNTY OF
I HEREBY CERTIFY that on this day before me, an officer duly qualified to take acknowledgments, personally appeared
{ YOUR NAME HERE }, who has produced _____ as identification and who executed the foregoing instrument and he/she acknowledged before me that he/she executed the same.
WITNESS my hand and official seal in the County and State aforesaid this _____ day of _____2016.

_____ Notary Public
Printed Name
My commission expires:

-------------------End of Letter.

Identification Form GENERATION 6.0 LETTER

Credit Repair is very specialized in many situations. If you need personal guidance on a specific issue you can call me. My phone number and information is on **PAGE 156.**
My Experience: Finance Degree, 6 years loans officer at a national bank, 4 1/2 years credit bureau manager for one of the big three credit bureau's   John D. Harris

Copy Driver's License

Bill addressed to you

Pay check stub with your address on it

On the bottom of this   "ID DOCUMENT"

I declare under penalty of perjury (under the laws of the United States of America) that this identification provide is me
John Doe
Signature
Date

Now your letter is ready to send. You will send your letter WITH TRACKING Priority Mail. This is your proof that CRA's get your letter(s).

This is an absolute must.

File all your paperwork.

Filling Your Complaint

You will have file complaint here:

Credit Repair is very specialized in many situations. If you need personal guidance on a specific issue you can call me. My phone number and information is on **PAGE 156.**

 My Experience: Finance Degree, 6 years loans officer at a national bank, 4 1/2 years credit bureau manager for one of the big three credit bureau's   John D. Harris

www.consumerfinance.gov/Complaint/

scan all your documents sent to the bureaus and there responses. You will be able to upload them.

Disputing With The Original Debtor

BEFORE DISPUTING WITH THE ORIGINAL CREDITOR YOU MUST HAVE DISPUTED WITH THE CREDIT BUREAUS .

How to Dispute Listing with Original Creditor

Creditors are the companies who initially reported your account to the credit bureaus and many times they have no record of your account at all. By law they have to remove your account if this is the case and have no proof.

Here is the exact statute in the FCRA:

§ 623. (a)(8) ABILITY OF CONSUMER TO DISPUTE INFORMATION DIRECTLY WITH FURNISHER

(A) IN GENERAL The Federal banking agencies, the National Credit Union Administration, and the Commission shall jointly prescribe regulations that shall identify the circumstances under which a furnisher shall be required to reinvestigate a dispute concerning the accuracy of information contained in a consumer report on the consumer, based on a direct request of a consumer.

(B) CONSIDERATIONS - In prescribing regulations under subparagraph (A), the agencies shall weigh--

(i) the benefits to consumers with the costs on furnishers and the credit reporting system;

(ii) the impact on the overall accuracy and integrity of consumer reports of any such requirements;

(iii) whether direct contact by the consumer with the furnisher would likely result in the most expeditious resolution of any such dispute; and

(iv) the potential impact on the credit reporting process if credit repair organizations, as defined in section 403(3), including entities that would be a credit repair organization, but for section 403(3)(B)(i), are able to circumvent the prohibition in subparagraph (G).

(C) APPLICABILITY Subparagraphs (D) through (G) shall apply in any circumstance identified under the regulations promulgated under subparagraph (A).

(D) SUBMITTING A NOTICE OF DISPUTE- A consumer who seeks to dispute the accuracy of information shall provide a dispute notice directly to such person at the address specified by the person for such notices that--

(i) identifies the specific information that is being disputed;

(ii) explains the basis for the dispute; and

(iii) includes all supporting documentation required by the furnisher to substantiate the basis of the dispute.

(E) DUTY OF PERSON AFTER RECEIVING NOTICE OF DISPUTE- After receiving a notice of dispute from a consumer pursuant to subparagraph (D), the person that provided the information in dispute to a consumer reporting agency shall--

(i) conduct an investigation with respect to the disputed information;

(ii) review all relevant information provided by the consumer with the notice;

(iii) complete such person's investigation of the dispute and report the results of the investigation to the consumer before the expiration of the period under section 611(a)(1) within which a consumer reporting agency would be required to complete its action if the consumer had elected to dispute the information under that section; and

(iv) if the investigation finds that the information reported was inaccurate, promptly notify each consumer reporting agency to which the person furnished the inaccurate information of that determination and provide to the agency any correction to that information that is necessary to make the information provided by the person accurate.

(F) FRIVOLOUS OR IRRELEVANT DISPUTE-

(i) IN GENERAL- This paragraph shall not apply if the person receiving a notice of a dispute from a consumer reasonably determines that the dispute is frivolous or irrelevant,

including--

(I) by reason of the failure of a consumer to provide sufficient information to investigate the disputed information; or

(II) the submission by a consumer of a dispute that is substantially the same as a dispute previously submitted by or for the consumer, either directly to the person or through a consumer reporting agency under subsection (b), with respect to which the person has already performed the person's duties under this paragraph or subsection (b), as applicable.

(ii) NOTICE OF DETERMINATION - Upon making any determination under clause (i) that a dispute is frivolous or irrelevant, the person shall notify the consumer of such determination not later than 5 business days after making such determination, by mail or, if authorized by the consumer for that purpose, by any other means available to the person.

(iii) CONTENTS OF NOTICE - A notice under clause (ii) shall include--

(I) the reasons for the determination under clause (i); and

(II) identification of any information required to investigate the disputed information, which may consist of a standardized form describing the general nature of such information.

and

§ 623. (b) Duties of furnishers of information upon notice of dispute.

(1) In general. After receiving notice pursuant to section 611(a)(2) [§ 1681i] of a dispute with regard to the completeness or accuracy of any information provided by a person to a consumer reporting agency, the person shall

(A) conduct an investigation with respect to the disputed information;

(B) review all relevant information provided by the consumer reporting agency pursuant to section 611(a)(2) [§ 1681i];

(C) report the results of the investigation to the consumer reporting agency;

(D) if the investigation finds that the information is incomplete or inaccurate, report those results to all other consumer reporting agencies to which the person furnished the information and that compile and maintain files on consumers on a nationwide basis; and

(E) if an item of information disputed by a consumer is found to be inaccurate or incomplete or cannot be verified after any reinvestigation under paragraph (1), for purposes of reporting to a consumer reporting agency only, as appropriate, based on the results of the reinvestigation promptly --

(i) modify that item of information;

(ii) delete that item of information; or

(iii) permanently block the reporting of that item of information.

In Layman's Terms

Now that your head is spinning with all that law, here is what is really means.

Basically, you can dispute information placed on your credit report by an original creditor in the same way as you would with a credit bureau. An original creditor must do the following.

Conduct an investigation of the dispute.

Review all information provided by the consumer relating to the dispute.

Respond within 30 days to the investigation.

If the information is inaccurate, they must notify the credit bureaus of the mistake and tell the credit bureau to correct it.

However, the creditor can also determine the dispute is frivolous just like a credit bureau can. Some reasons as to why a dispute may be frivolous.

You just disputed the same thing without changing the reason for the dispute.

You haven't provided enough information for the creditor to conduct an investigation. At the minimum, you need to identify the account by account number and provide a reason why you are disputing.

If the creditor does determine the dispute is frivolous, they must notify you in writing by any other means available to the person within 5 days.

If the Creditor Fails to Comply with the Law

If the original creditor fails to comply with your dispute, they are in violation of the FCRA, but you can't sue them unless you have disputed with the Credit Bureaus first.

Disputing with the credit bureau first is not something you can shortcut or forget. In order to place the liability of reporting accurately squarely on the shoulders of the creditor, you must have disputed the listing with the credit bureaus. This means you have either online, via the telephone or in writing, disputed a listing with the credit bureaus and then WAITED FOR THE RESULTS OF THE INVESTIGATION.

Here is the law which enforces the fact that you must dispute with the credit bureau first:

§ 623. (c) LIMITATION ON LIABILITY- Except as provided in section 621(c)(1)(B), sections 616 and 617 do not apply to any violation of--

(1) subsection (a) of this section, including any regulations issued thereunder;

(2) subsection (e) of this section, except that nothing in this paragraph shall limit, expand, or otherwise affect liability under section 616 or 617, as applicable, for violations of subsection (b) of this section;

Sections 616 and 617 of the FCRA talk about how much the fines are for violations of the FCRA (the willful and negligent non compliance), typically $1,000.

What the above section of the FCRA § 623(c) means is that if you dispute with the original creditors first, without having disputing through the credit bureaus, and they refuse to answer you, or provide you with proof, yes, they are in violation of the FCRA, but you as a private citizen cannot take them to court and sue them; only your state authorities (like your state attorney general) or federal authorities (like the FTC) can sue them.

However, if you have disputed the information with the credit bureaus first, they are supposed to have talked to the original creditor, even though we know that doesn't happen, and the original creditor is supposed to have at that time conducted an investigation, under FCRA § 623(b), under which you, as a private citizen can sue them. When you go to the original creditor under FCRA § 623(a)(8), you are just merely asking for the OC's proof that they must have provided to the credit bureaus during the OC's thorough investigation. If they have no proof of negative information, but the credit bureau says that the results of the investigation show the negative information is accurate, then you have the OC on an actionable, sue-able (by you) offense.

Once again, YOU MUST DISPUTE WITH THE CREDIT BUREAUS FIRST - Have we said this often enough??

Steps to Dispute with Original Creditor

What is the exact procedure when you want to dispute things with the original creditor? The Steps:

Dispute the listing with the credit bureau.

Wait for the results of the investigation.

If the listing is deleted or modified per your desires, you're done!

If the information furnisher does not get back to you within 30 days:

You need to send a letter to the company's legal department informing them they are in violation of the FCRA and you intend to sue if they do not remove the listing.

If they do not remove the listing, you will have to sue if you want to get it off.

If the information furnisher says the results of the investigation is verified, then:

Call up the credit card company and ask them what kind of documentation they have to prove the negative mark. Many times they will have nothing.

Letter to the Original Debtor

Your Name
Address

Credit Repair is very specialized in many situations. If you need personal guidance on a specific issue you can call me. My phone number and information is on **PAGE 156**.

My Experience: Finance Degree, 6 years loans officer at a national bank, 4 1/2 years credit bureau manager for one of the big three credit bureau's   John D. Harris

City, State

Zip

SSN: 000-00-0000 | DOB: 1/1/1970

Bank of America

P.O. Box 4568

Dallas, TX 75013

Dear Legal Department:

Re: Acct #XXXXXXXX

This letter is in regards to a phone call I placed to your company regarding the account listed above on <Insert Date>.

I called to inquire about this account that is listed on my Credit Reports. I spoke to **<Insert Customer Service Representative named>** and her employee number is **<Insert #>**, as provided by her. She informed me that your company does not have any information on this account that it was all sent to a collection agency. How did you investigate this account without any documentation? I contacted the collection agency your rep told me about and they could not validate the debt. This collection agency subsequently removed all information regarding this account from my credit reports. If this incorrect information is not removed from my credit reports, I will file suit against your company.

First Name

Last Name

Email

Phone

Zip Code

IN WITNESS WHEREOF, the said party has signed and sealed these presents the day and year first above written. Signed, sealed and delivered in the presence of:

{PRINT YOUR NAME HERE} _____ Signature

STATE OF

COUNTY OF

I HEREBY CERTIFY that on this day before me, an officer duly qualified to take acknowledgments, personally appeared

{   YOUR   NAME   HERE   },   who   has   produced

_____   as   identification   and   who executed the foregoing instrument and he/she acknowledged before me that he/she executed the same.

WITNESS my hand and official seal in the County and State aforesaid this _____ day of _____2016.

_____ Notary Public

Printed Name

My commission expires:

Identification Form

Copy Driver's License

Bill addressed to you

Pay check stub with your address on it

On the bottom of this "ID DOCUMENT"

I declare under penalty of perjury (under the laws of the United States of America) that this identification provide is me
John Doe
Signature
Date

Credit Repair is very specialized in many situations. If you need personal guidance on a specific issue you can call me. My phone number and information is on **PAGE 156.**

My Experience: Finance Degree, 6 years loans officer at a national bank, 4 1/2 years credit bureau manager for one of the big three credit bureau's   John D. Harris

Credit Repair is very specialized in many situations. If you need personal guidance on a specific issue you can call or email me.

You can email me at creditdisputeletterbible@yahoo.com

If you want to call me you can at: 1-800-373-1093

Push #2 on your phone.   You can add funds to your phone number.

I charge $2.99 a minute. Most cases can be solved in 10 minutes.

After you add funds my extension is 31843

I ANSWER ALL CALLS MYSELF.

My Experience: Finance Degree, 6 years loans officer at a national bank, 4 1/2 years credit bureau manager for one of the big three credit bureau's   John D. Harris

Credit Repair is very specialized in many situations. If you need personal guidance on a specific issue you can call or email me.

You can email me at creditdisputeletterbible@yahoo.com

If you want to call me you can at: 1-800-373-1093

Push #2 on your phone.   You can add funds to your phone number.

I charge $2.99 a minute. Most cases can be solved in 10 minutes.

After you add funds my extension is 31843

I ANSWER ALL CALLS MYSELF.

My Experience: Finance Degree, 6 years loans officer at a national bank, 4 1/2 years credit bureau manager for one of the big three credit bureau's   John D. Harris

Credit Repair is very specialized in many situations. If you need personal guidance on a specific issue you can call me. My phone number and information is on **PAGE 156.**

 My Experience: Finance Degree, 6 years loans officer at a national bank, 4 1/2 years credit bureau manager for one of the big three credit bureau's   John D. Harris

www.ingramcontent.com/pod-product-compliance
Lightning Source LLC
Chambersburg PA
CBHW070242190526
45169CB00001B/278